Rereadings

Rereadings

Edited by

ANNE FADIMAN

Farrar, Straus and Giroux   *New York*

Farrar, Straus and Giroux
19 Union Square West, New York 10003

These essays originally appeared, in slightly different form, in
The American Scholar.

The excerpt from the interview with Christina Stead originally appeared in
A Writing Life: Interviews with Australian Women Writers *by*
Giulia Giuffrè (Allen & Unwin, 1990) and is reprinted courtesy of the author.

Library of Congress Cataloging-in-Publication Data
Rereadings / edited by Anne Fadiman.— 1st ed.
   p. cm.
   Essays previously published in The American scholar, the journal of
the Phi Beta Kappa Society.
   ISBN-13: 978-0-374-24942-7
   ISBN-10: 0-374-24942-3 (pbk. : alk. paper)
   1. Authors, American—Books and reading.   I. Fadiman, Anne, 1953–

Z1039.A87R47 2005
028'.9—dc22

                                        2005040018

Designed by Jonathan D. Lippincott

www.fsgbooks.com

1   3   5   7   9   10   8   6   4   2

For John Bethell,
teacher then and now

CONTENTS

Foreword: On Rereading

hen my son was eight, I read C. S. Lewis's *The Horse and His Boy* aloud to him. I had originally read it when I was eight myself, and although I'd reread the better-known Narnia books—*The Lion, the Witch and the Wardrobe*; *The Magician's Nephew*; *The Silver Chair*—in the interim, more than forty years had passed since I'd read *The Horse and His Boy*.

Reading a favorite book to your child is one of the most pleasurable forms of rereading, provided the child's enthusiasm is equal to yours and thus gratifyingly validates your literary taste, your parental competence, and your own former self. Henry loved *The Horse and His Boy*, the tale of two children and two talking horses who gallop across an obstacle-fraught desert in hopes of averting the downfall of an imperiled kingdom that lies to the north. It's the most suspenseful of the Narnia books, and Henry, who was at that poignant age when parents are still welcome at bedtime but can glimpse their banishment on the horizon, begged me each night not to turn out the light just yet: how about another page, and then how about another paragraph, and then, come on, how about just one more *sentence*? There was only one problem with this idyllic picture. As I read the book to Henry, I was thinking to myself that C. S. Lewis, not to put too fine a point on it, was a racist and sexist pig.

I'd read two biographies of Lewis and knew that his relations with women, colored by the death of his mother when he was nine, were pretty peculiar. I'd read "The Shoddy Lands," a creepy misogynist fantasy in which the (male) narrator encounters a giantess whose nude body makes him gag. However, I remembered *The Horse and His Boy* only as a rollicking equestrian adventure, sort of like *Misty of Chincoteague* but with swordfights instead of Pony Penning Day. My jaw dropped when I realized that Aravis, its heroine, is acceptable to Lewis because she acts like a boy—she's interested in "bows and arrows and horses and dogs and swimming"—and even dresses like one, whereas the book's only girly girl, a devotee of "clothes and parties and gossip," is an object of contempt. Even more appalling was Lewis's treatment of the Calormenes, a brown-skinned people who wear turbans and carry scimitars. (Forty years ago, the crude near-homonym had slipped by me. This time around, I wondered briefly if Lewis was thinking only about climate—*calor* is Latin for "heat"—but decided that was unlikely. It's as if he'd named a Chinese character Mr. Yellow: it had to be on purpose.) The book's hero, Shasta, is the ward of a venial Calormene fisherman, but, as a visitor observes, "this boy is manifestly no son of yours, for your cheek is as dark as mine but the boy is fair and white." That's how we know he belongs to a noble northern race instead of an uncouth southern one. Of the Calormene capital—the seat of a fat, obnoxious, vulgarly bejeweled potentate called the Tisroc— Lewis remarks that "what you would chiefly have noticed if you had been there was the smells, which came from unwashed people, unwashed dogs, scent, garlic, onions, and the piles of refuse which lay everywhere."

It was difficult to read this kind of thing to Henry without comment: the words, after all, were coming to him in *my voice.* I held my tongue for the first hundred pages or so, but finally I blurted out, "Have you noticed that *The Horse and His Boy* isn't really fair to girls? And that all the bad guys have dark skin?"

Henry considered this seriously for a moment. "That's not true," he said. "The Tisroc is a bad guy, and C. S. Lewis doesn't say *he* has dark skin."

"Well, he's a Calormene, and all the Calormenes are dark. Of course"—I could hear myself start to fumble— "fifty years ago, when this book was written, lots of people had ideas that weren't true, about whether boys were better than girls, or whites were better than blacks, or—"

Henry shot me the sort of look he might have used had I dumped a pint of vinegar into a bowl of chocolate ice cream. And who could blame him? He didn't want to analyze, criticize, evaluate, or explicate the book. He didn't want to size it up or slow it down. He wanted exactly what I had wanted at eight: to find out if Shasta and Aravis would get to Archenland in time to warn King Lune that his castle was about to be attacked by evil Prince Rabadash and two hundred Calormene horsemen. "Mommy," he said fiercely, "can you just *read?*"

And there lay the essential differences between reading and rereading, acts that Henry and I were performing simultaneously. The former had more velocity; the latter had more depth. The former shut out the world in order to focus on the story; the latter dragged in the world in order to assess the story. The former was more fun; the latter was more cynical. But what was remarkable about the latter was that it *contained* the former: even while, as with the upper half of a set of bifocals, I saw the book through the complicating lens of adulthood, I also saw it through the memory of the first time I'd read it, when it had seemed as swift and pure as the Winding Arrow, the river that divides Calormen from Archenland.

Eight years ago, when I became editor of the literary quarterly *The American Scholar*, one of the first tasks I faced was how to organize the books department. Of course we needed to review recently published books, but how could we also honor the fact that for all true readers, the bonds that count are not with books we haven't yet met but with those we already know intimately? As the poet Austin Dobson observed in 1908, new books "have neither part nor lot in our past of retrospect and suggestion. Of what we were, of what we like or liked, they know nothing; and we—if that be possible—

know even less of them." The solution was so obvious I wondered why every magazine didn't do it: we'd open our books section with an essay not on reading something new but on rereading something old.

And thus these Rereadings were born. In each issue of the *Scholar*, a distinguished writer chose a book (or a story or a poem or even, in one case, an album cover) that had made an indelible impression on him or her before the age of twenty-five and reread it at thirty or fifty or seventy. The object of the writer's affections might be famous or obscure; a venerated classic or a piece of beloved trash; a fairy tale read as a child, a novel read in the throes of first love, a reference work that guided the early stages of a career.

In short order the Rereadings became the most popular part of the magazine. Perhaps that is because they weren't conventional literary criticism; they were about relationships. The relationship between reader and book, like all relationships that matter, changes over time. A book that seemed a fount of wisdom to a fifteen-year-old might seem a trough of hogwash to a fifty-year-old; on the other hand, passages that were once dull or incomprehensible might be transformed by life experience from dross into gold. The Rereadings, as it turned out, revealed at least as much about the readers as about the books. Each was a miniature memoir at whose heart lay that most galvanic of topics, the evolving nature of love. Even if decades had passed, many of the writers remembered the color of the original book cover, the chair they'd sat in, the season, the time of day. *Of course* they did! Don't you remember the room in which you lay with your first lover, the way the bed faced, the color of the sheets, whether the pillows were soft or lumpy?

This book contains my seventeen favorite Rereadings: favorite not just because they're so good but because they're so dissimilar. Though all the writers are American, they live in five different countries; the books they write about represent eight nationalities. Their perspectives, their literary styles, and their senses of humor are as variegated as a patchwork quilt assembled partly from Balenciaga gowns, partly from torn blue jeans. But all of these essays pursue the same fugitive quarry—the nature of reading—and, taken together, they have helped me understand why the reader who plucks a book from her shelf only once is as deprived as the listener who, after attending a single performance of a Beethoven symphony, never hears it again.

According to that peerless rereader Holbrook Jackson, the Reverend Alexander Scott read Carlyle's *French Revolution* four times; Edward FitzGerald read Richardson's *Clarissa* five times; John Stuart Mill read Pope's translations of the *Iliad* and the *Odyssey* at least twenty times; and *The Times* of London, in 1928, reported the existence of a society "for which a twenty-fifth reading of 'Esmond' was the necessary qualification of membership." Much as I admire Thackeray, I suspect that the members of that society experienced diminishing returns.

The first time, especially if it's in childhood, is induplicable. It is customary to speak of children as vessels into which

books are poured, but I think the reverse analogy is more ac-
curate: children pour themselves into books, changing their
shape to fit each vessel. "I have been Tom Jones," said David
Copperfield; he was also Roderick Random and, armed with
the centerpiece of an old set of boot trees, "Captain Somebody,
of the Royal British Navy, in danger of being beset by savages, and resolved to sell his life at a great price." We haven't
become ourselves yet, so we try on literary identities, fantastic at first and then closer and closer to home. Am I more like
Mole or like Toad? I asked myself at six, undeterred by such
trifling details as size and species. At eight, when gender was
still no barrier: Aravis or Shasta? At sixteen: Dorothea or
Rosamond? I think that's why so many children prefer fiction
and so many adults prefer nonfiction. As we age, we coagulate.
Our shapes become fixed and we can no longer be poured.

Tom Jones also left its mark on William Hazlitt. In "On
Reading Old Books," the greatest essay on rereading I know,
Hazlitt wrote:

> It came down in numbers once a fortnight, in Cooke's pocket-
> edition, embellished with cuts. I had hitherto read only in
> school-books, and a tiresome ecclesiastical history (with the
> exception of Mrs. Radcliffe's *Romance of the Forest*): but this
> had a different relish with it,—"sweet in the mouth," though
> not "bitter in the belly." It smacked of the world I lived in, and
> in which I was to live.

How wonderful to think of a time when *Tom Jones* wasn't
an English-class assignment but the most exciting escape-
reading imaginable! The edition Hazlitt mentions cost six-
pence and was published serially, leaving him hanging "just

in the middle of a sentence, and in the nick of a story, where Tom Jones discovers Square behind the blanket." It came out in 1792, forty-three years after the book's original publication, so Hazlitt would have been fourteen, just the age at which a certain kind of smart, imaginative, and (for the time being) unhappy child gets along better with the characters in his library than with his peers. His pores are open; he is painfully impressionable; his enjoyment of literature is enhanced not by knowledge but by ignorance. Hazlitt understood this perfectly:

> A sage philosopher, who was not a very wise man, said, that he should like very well to be young again, if he could take his experience along with him. This ingenious person did not seem to be aware, by the gravity of his remark, that the great advantage of being young is to be without this weight of experience, which he would fain place upon the shoulders of youth, and which never comes too late with years. Oh! what a privilege to be able to let this hump, like Christian's burthen, drop from off one's back, and transport oneself, by the help of a little musty duodecimo [a pocket-size book], to the time when "ignorance was bliss," and when we first got a peep at the raree-show of the world, through the glass of fiction.

From a child's vantage, the literary raree-show often seems more full of life than life itself. Perhaps that is why most young readers are more interested in characters than in authors. Thinking about the act of composition—of people grinding out marketable sentences like bakers assembling cheese danishes—forces them to acknowledge that the characters were made up. They know that, of course, but they'd rather not have their noses rubbed in it. They'll be taking up

Christian's burthen (a reference to the heavy load the ragged hero of *Pilgrim's Progress* carries on his back) soon enough.

The problem with being ravished by books at an early age is that later rereadings are often likely to disappoint. "The sharp luscious flavor, the fine *aroma* is fled," Hazlitt wrote, "and nothing but the stalk, the bran, the husk of literature is left." Terrible words, but it can happen. You become harder to move, frighten, arouse, provoke, jangle. Your education becomes an interrogation lamp under which the hapless book, its every wart and scar exposed, confesses its guilty secrets: "My characters are wooden! My plot creaks! I am pre-feminist, pre-deconstructivist, and pre-postcolonialist!" (The upside of English classes is that they give you critical tools, some of which are useful, but the downside is that those tools make you less able to shower your books with unconditional love. Conditions are the very thing you're asked to learn.) You read too many *other* books, and the currency of each one becomes debased.

Is rereading, then, doomed to be an exercise in disillusionment, letdown, loss? Of course not. Sometimes the book may be so great that familiarity enlarges it rather than diminishes it; it expands like the chambers of a nautilus, growing as you grow. Nobody has ever said, "Gee, *War and Peace* seemed kind of thin the second time around." Or it may be so difficult that it simply can't be assimilated all at once. When I read my first Shakespeare play—*A Midsummer Night's Dream*, at twelve—I was exhausted by the time I'd located the subjects and verbs and had little energy left for such niceties as plot and character. Or on the first go-round you may get it *wrong*. When I read Robert Browning's "My Last Duchess" at thirteen, I didn't understand that the narrator had murdered his wife; that's the whole point of the poem, but it was like invisible ink, legible only on rereading. Or maybe the book is about something you haven't yet experienced—love, parenthood, vocation—and until you reread it fifteen years later, all you can do is press your nose against the glass.

One of the strongest motivations for rereading is purely selfish: it helps you remember what you used to be like. Open an old paperback, spangled with marginalia in a handwriting you outgrew long ago, and memories will jump out with as much vigor as if you'd opened your old diary. These book-memories, says Hazlitt, are "pegs and loops on which we can hang up, or from which we can take down, at pleasure, the wardrobe of a moral imagination, the relics of our best affections, the tokens and records of our happiest hours." Or our unhappiest. Rereading forces you to spend time, at claustrophobically close range, with your earnest, anxious, pretentious, embarrassing former self, a person you thought you had left behind but who turns out to have been living inside you all along.

If a book read when young is a lover, that same book, reread later on, is a friend: "the best of friends," wrote the Victorian artist William James Linton, "That cannot be estranged or take offence / Howe'er neglected, but returns at

will / With the old friendship." This may sound like a de-
motion, but after all, it is old friends, not old lovers, to whom
you are most likely to turn when you need comfort. Fatigue,
grief, and illness call for familiarity, not innovation. In bed
with the flu, you do not say, "Hey, I've never tried Afghan
food! Let's order some takeout, and heavy on the turmeric!"
You crave chicken soup. Similarly, you're likely to crave a
book you know well, perhaps a slightly childish one that
will countenance a soothing regression. Down from the shelf
comes *Jane Eyre*. Jane is the perfect visitor: her bedside
manners are excellent, her conversation isn't too taxing, and
her dependable progress toward a happy ending sets an example for your recovery.

The words reread at a vulnerable moment, however, need
not always be easy or cheerful. Four months before he died,
Alfred Kazin, whose work I'd published in *The American
Scholar*, wrote me a letter that concluded:

> Yesterday, sick at heart at the struggle with my 82-year-old
> body as I fought a violent cold rainstorm, I finally got home,
> picked up Hardy's poems and read myself back to life, as it
> were, thanks to his gift for putting one back into the whole de-
> sign of life and death. No false optimism there, but what brac-
> ing truth in the very lilt of the words.

Hardy? Under those circumstances I might have chosen a
jollier companion than the man who wrote, "We are old; /
These younger press; we feel our rout / Is imminent to Aïdes'
den,— / That evening shades are stretching out, /

•

Gentlemen!" But I have little doubt that Hardy was exactly the friend that Kazin needed.

After my truncated exchange with Henry, it took us another couple of weeks to finish reading The Horse and His Boy. Parts of it were very beautiful: the night that Shasta spends at the Tombs of the Ancient Kings; the day that Aravis, wounded and exhausted, spends in the stone house of the Hermit of the Southern March, lying on a bed of heather. I liked the way the Hermit sportscasts the great battle at the end of the book: "Lune and Azrooh are fighting hand to hand; the King looks like winning—the King is keeping it up well—the King has won. Azrooh's down. King Edmund's down—no, he's up again: he's at it with Rabadash . . ." Even though I knew it was coming, I savored the moment when Shasta, who had been kidnapped in infancy, is revealed to be a prince. I was charmed by the resolution of the main characters' relationship, which seemed less misogynistic than refreshingly antiromantic: "Aravis also had many quarrels (and, I'm afraid, even fights) with [Shasta], but they always made it up again: so that years later, when they were grown up, they were so used to quarrelling and making it up again that they got married so as to go on doing it more conveniently."

Still, C. S. Lewis treated girls and Calormenes as inferiors, and I could not get that out of my mind. For a while, the knowledge of his small-mindedness wrestled uneasily with the pleasure I took in his book. By the time I closed the last page, however, I found that the pleasure, without conscious instruction from me though doubtless with some abetment by Henry, had clearly gotten the upper hand. The book's flaws were serious, but the connection was too strong to sever.

And why shouldn't it be? The same thing happens with our parents. They start out as gods, and then we learn that they committed adultery, or drank too much, or cheated on their taxes, or maybe they just looked awkward on the dance floor or went on too long when they told a story. But do we stop loving them?

A.F.

Rereadings

Marginal Notes on the Inner Lives of People with Cluttered Apartments in the East Seventies

Franny and Zooey, by J. D. Salinger

o one becomes a reader except in answer to some baffling inner necessity, of the kind that leads people to turn cartwheels outside the 7-Eleven, jump headlong through a plate-glass window, join the circus, or buy a low-end foreign car when the nearest appropriate auto-repair shop is fifty miles away. With these dramatic examples fresh in your mind, you'll probably require only a small amount of additional convincing that my little theory—based on years of painful experience—is true. Reading requires a loner's temperament, a high tolerance for silence, and an unhealthy preference for the company of people who are imaginary or dead.

It also requires patience, or what my high-school gym teacher, whose name I remember as Randy Fisk, or Fist—a bantamweight Irishman with a ginger mustache, who exhibited a suspicious delight in watching his fourteen-year-old charges vault a padded "horse"—used to call "good old-fashioned stick-to-itiveness." His opinion was that readers were pale unnatural freaks with a built-in resistance to normal physical exercise. And because, like so many freaks, I have a desperate desire to appear normal, it pains me to admit that Mr. Fist, or Fisk, was right. Readers are freaks. There is really no way to deny it.

The comparison between readers and writers on this score is instructive. While writers have historically made a point of displaying themselves as unusually sensitive, troubled souls (see Verlaine, Rimbaud, Thomas Wolfe, Plath, Burroughs, Ginsberg, et al.; note that most of the truly crazy ones are poets), it is also my theory that their dramatic sufferings are very often the product of too much ambition. Too much actual, organic suffering in one's biography can make it impossible to sustain the energy and egotism necessary for a successful literary career. A career of reading, on the other hand, allows for more prolonged and spectacular forms of disturbance. It is no accident, at least, that most readers I know were unhappy children. They spent months in the hospital; endured long periods of friendlessness or bereavement; watched loved ones die of cancer; had parents who were crazy or divorced; spent formative years in a foreign country; suffered from early exposure to "fantasy" or "adventure" novels for boys or "mystery" or "romance" novels for girls; or lived through some overwhelming experience of dislocating weirdness, such as growing up on an army base, or on a farm, or in a cult.

My own reasons for bookishness are less dramatic. There were the stresses of a home where my unhappy parents fought all the time, inculcating in me a very natural desire to escape from reality. But the greatest injury I suffered was the absence of a television set, which cut me off from the comforting stream of voices, pictures, characters, and stories in which my peers ritually immersed themselves every day after school. Assigned the role of Gilligan from *Gilligan's Island*, I remember standing on our asphalt playground in Brooklyn without the slightest idea of what to say or how to behave. After school, I went home and read books. It was less boring than staring up at the ceiling or listening to my parents fight.

By the age of fifteen, I was a full-time reader. I hid books under my desk. I read in the library after school. Reading was an escape from the crushing pressures of adolescence, such as speaking out loud in class or making direct eye contact with my peers in the halls. Books were a promise that I might at least learn to impersonate someone normal. I loved *The Great Gatsby*. If Gatsby himself was blurry and suspicious, Nick Carraway was the kind of friend I would have liked to have. Hemingway was good, particularly the early stories (how to talk to hoboes and boxers). Flaubert was great, particularly *Sentimental Education* (Madame Bovary reminded me of my mother). While Edith Wharton had a wonderful eye for details, I could never understand how she chose her main characters. Reading her books was like watching a brilliant hostess in her drawing room making witty observations to dullards and bores. Why she invited these people over was beyond me. Henry James was worse. Virginia Woolf was a great writer. Still, it didn't escape my attention that Septimus Smith threw himself out a window; or that

Leonard Bast, my favorite character from Woolf's great pre-decessor E. M. Forster, was crushed to death by a shelf of books. Woolf and Forster were snobs. Of the "modern" American writers, John Updike was like Flaubert, except he used his terrific skill to convince the reader that he actually liked Rabbit Angstrom, whereas the Updike I imagined (namely, me) would have been delighted when Rabbit's life turned mediocre and unhappy. Philip Roth was too close to home.

More than any of the other famous writers I read, J. D. Salinger actively courted my adolescent longings and fantasies, particularly when it came to the dreamlike specificity of his highly desirable Manhattan interiors. In *Franny and Zooey*, the author speaks through Buddy Glass, a writer who admired *The Great Gatsby*, "which was my 'Tom Sawyer' when I was twelve," and whose main business, as far as I could make out, was dispensing cracker-barrel wisdom like an old-timer at the track. Buddy was also happy to share the insider details I craved, namely, the wall hangings, reading habits, vocal inflections, and bathroom-medicine-cabinet contents of a family of precocious, sensitive, unhappy children who lived on the Upper East Side of Manhattan. (My family lived in Brooklyn, then moved to New Jersey when I was nine. Manhattan was a dream. The mental Post-it I attached to *Franny and Zooey* reads something like "Notes on the Inner Lives of People with Cluttered Apartments in the East Seventies.") It was encouraging to know that my yearnings for a guide through the darkness of this world were answered by the tender proclivities (which now seem stranger and darker but no less affecting) of the famous author of *The Catcher in the Rye*, a novel that played on self-pitying adolescent instincts without offering any useful wisdom in return. Seymour Glass would have hated it. (It is no accident, I believe, that both John Hinckley, Jr., and Mark David Chapman were carrying copies of Salinger's little red book when they shot Ronald Reagan and John Lennon, respectively.)

Between the ages of fourteen and twenty-four I read *Franny and Zooey* from cover to cover at least five times. I underlined passages and made cryptic notations in the margins, hoping to become a better person (witty, literate, living in Manhattan), an acceptable character free from the bipolar alternation of uncontrolled aggression and sad passivity that I saw in my parents' marriage and was only beginning to recognize in myself.

By relating this mishmash of biographical details in a jaded, older-person voice, I hardly mean to suggest that reading was not a worthwhile habit. Nor do I intend to explain away, through an act of knowing posthumous revisitation, the failings of my fourteen-year-old self (who, by the way, deserves tons of sympathy and understanding, but whom I have little interest, should the opportunity somehow present itself, in ever meeting again: his unhappiness, his eagerness to please, and his frantic desire to escape from his family give him all the retrospective charm of a small ferret trapped in a corner). What bothers me about him has nothing to do with his aesthetic sense. It is his lack of any real capacity to enter sympathetically into the minds of other people. I read books in order to learn how to be the *right* kind of character in the *right* kind of novel. The authors of these novels were people (by "people" I meant people who were confident and knowing, i.e., *rich people*, or characters like Nick Carraway, who were accepted by the rich) who had condescended to share their knowledge. They were not people like my parents or me, who were anxious from morning through most of the afternoon, and at night were very often *scared to death*. It never occurred to me that the need to catalog the stuff of everyday life might be a sign that the authors I loved were loners and misfits. Normal people, after all, don't stand around at garden parties or lie in bed with their loved ones trying to figure out what even the smallest ordinary gesture *means*.

Franny and Zooey was different. It was my *Stover at Yale*. The wisdom that Salinger was interested in dispensing was more difficult than the simple stick-to-itiveness of Dink Stover (a step up from "striver") or my high-school gym teacher, Mr. Fisk, or Fist. I never felt much identity with such well-balanced characters anyway. I didn't know anyone who went to Yale. And if I wanted to be Dink Stover (a hero-athlete, admired by his peers), or even F. Scott Fitzgerald, I also knew that they were too far a reach. In *Franny and Zooey*, the Dink Stover character, waiting on the train platform in Princeton to receive Franny Glass, was called Lane Coutell. "Lane Coutell, in a Burberry raincoat that apparently had a wool liner buttoned into it, was one of the six or seven boys out on the open platform. Or, rather, he was and he wasn't one of them." Who doesn't feel like that? In the paperback *Franny* I owned at fourteen, and have read ever since, I underlined "he was and he wasn't one of them" twice in blue ink. The tip about the Burberry coat with the wool liner seemed useful too. (Did the Princeton men of 1984—the year of the Talking Heads' best album—still meet "dates" on train platforms wearing Burberry raincoats? I believed the answer was yes.)

Still, there was no getting around the fact that I was bad at sports and had trouble looking directly at other people in the halls. And J. D. Salinger knew it. He knew that his readers feared and resented the Lane Coutells of this world with all the force of the profound self-hatred that only adolescents can muster. And unlike Fitzgerald, or Hemingway, or the author of *Stover at Yale*, whose name doesn't seem particularly worth remembering, Salinger was on our side. "I've *missed* you," Franny tells Lane. The words are no sooner out of Franny's mouth, the author eagerly informs us, "than she realized that she didn't mean them at all."

That was how I felt about Lane too, and it was at this moment that my underlining became enthusiastic. It wasn't Lane we were supposed to like. It was Franny. Lane is a self-important snob, a charm boy, a gym-class standout who uses words like "testicularity" and then pretends that he said something else. Franny isn't fooled. And as she cuts him up, "with equal parts of self-disapproval and malice," Salinger is careful to keep the reader on her side by assuring us that her disdain is self-conscious and specific, and would never be extended to us. You don't have to hate yourself, I felt like telling Franny. Lane is an *asshole*.

Franny was blameless, brave, and falling apart. Also self-less and knowing. "I'm just sick of ego, ego, ego," she says. "My own and everybody else's." I underlined that line with a vengeance. "I'm afraid I *will* compete," one page later, was even better, rating both a five-pointed star *and* an exclamation point in blue. The underlined passages are obvious attempts to engage the sympathies of adolescent loners by telling a familiar story (Dink Stover at Yale) from the more original and appealing reverse angle (Franny, his date, who thinks he's a jerk). They worked. I was charmed. The specter of testicularity was ridiculed and banished. Despite her emotional condition, and the difference in our ages, I might even have considered asking Franny out on a date.

The centerpiece of the next section of the book is Buddy's letter to his younger brother Zooey. I confess that my fourteen- and even my twenty-year-old selves were never very interested in this letter. The writing was looser, stammering, written by a stand-up comic with sweaty palms and a brand-new routine, looking out into the dark. I didn't want to know about Buddy Glass. I wanted to know more about Franny. I was disturbed by Salinger's desire to shift the ground of his story, to break through the conventional demands of rewriting *Stover at Yale* or early Fitzgerald from a sly, sardonic angle and infuse the voice with a more self-conscious humor that underlined the vulnerability of his narrator—a person of adult years and experience who was willing to admit, in public, that he "burst into tears at the first harsh or remonstrative word." I knew that line was a joke. (I wrote "joke" in blue ink in the margin.) Still, it was the kind of joke that made me nervous. Entering into a pact of sympathetic understanding with such a person, I knew, was unwise.

On my second reading, at age seventeen or eighteen, I found Buddy's sense of humor more sympathetic. I liked "if my Muses failed to provide for me, I'd go grind lenses somewhere, like Booker T. Washington." I was proud of myself for getting why the comparison between Buddy Glass and the author of *Up from Slavery* was funny. ("Unexpected," I wrote, in pedantic red ink. "*Not* Benjamin Franklin.") I also appreciated the description of Les Glass, later on in the book, as "an inveterate and wistful admirer of the wall décor at Sardi's theatrical restaurant." I underlined the phrase "theatrical restaurant," because it was the addition of those two words to "Sardi's" that made the joke work.

Funny or not, Buddy Glass—from the perspective of age fourteen, and age seventeen or eighteen, and even age twenty—was never as interesting as his dead brother Seymour, who left behind a deceptively simple three-line koan whose meaning tantalized and captivated me for ten years without ever quite becoming clear: "The little girl on the plane / Who turned her doll's head around / To look at me." Because Seymour Glass plays only a ghostly Jamesian role in *Franny and Zooey*, it seems wrong to go into my idealization of him here. Why did Seymour kill himself? Was the beauty of the little girl's gesture—is she trying to be *polite*, does she really think the doll is a *person*—not enough? Was it a protest against what the girl would become when she grew up? Or did the charming gesture contain the seeds of the adult corruption that would later destroy her soul? None of these questions can be answered within the text of *Franny and Zooey*. What's here is Buddy's practical advice to his brother: "*Act*, Zachary Martin Glass, when and where you want to, since you feel you must, but do it *with all your might.*"

Zachary Martin Glass, or Zooey, was my favorite character in the book. He is Seymour and Buddy's Zen teachings, he is the rebellion against those teachings, he is funny and handsome, he is an actor, and he even bears a passing resemblance to Lane Coutell. (Both are objects of adolescent male identification. The demographics are different, that's all.) If Buddy Glass made me uneasy, Zooey was a perfect stand-in. He is an airbrushed version of Buddy, a character any adolescent misfit would be happy to have as a friend, a proof of the benign and charitable intentions of his author. After twenty pages of Buddy Glass, I was happy to be finally alone with Zooey. Someone in this family was normal. At the same time, my feelings for Zooey contained a hard, uncomfortable kernel of self-hatred that never quite dissolved, no matter how many times I read the book.

But this piece of dishonesty was more than made up for by my favorite scene in the book, the bathroom scene between Zooey and his mother, Bessie Glass. Bessie is a classic. (Les Glass tap-dances his way into the text only twice, in a memory of a long-ago birthday party and as a semi-ghostly presence who proffers a tangerine to his disconsolate daughter.) She is a "svelte twilight soubrette . . . photographed . . . in her old housecoat." The sentence that follows a few pages later is worthy of Balzac, a real beauty. The subject is Bessie's housecoat:

> With its many occultish-looking folds, it also served as the repository for the paraphernalia of a very heavy cigarette smoker and an amateur handyman; two oversized pockets had been added at the hips, and they usually contained two or three packs of cigarettes, several match folders, a screwdriver, a claw-end hammer, a Boy Scout knife that had once belonged to one of her sons, and an enamel faucet handle or two, plus an assortment of screws, nails, hinges, and ball-bearing casters— all of which tended to make Mrs. Glass chink faintly as she moved about in her large apartment.

Slovenly, patched together, proceeding according to a purely comic logic, if by any logic at all, and stopping just short of the darker comedy of Beckett, Bessie's old housecoat is the best description of domestic memory that I know. Perhaps the ability to find meaning in that memory is ultimately what saves us. Salinger never quite agrees. (Zooey is exasperated. Bessie is a dope.) Still, he is willing to give Bessie and her housecoat their due.

The love scene between Bessie Glass and her son is the answer to the love scene between Franny and Lane in Princeton, and to the lousy television script that Zooey reads in the bath. They are honest with each other. "This is supposed to be a family of all adults," Bessie says. She is dumb as a post. But she knows that Franny is hurt and that she can't fix it. And just when the scene might get sentimental, Buddy steps in to let us know that the eyes that used to announce the tragedy of her two dead sons now tear up with the announcement that some remote Hollywood starlet's marriage is on the rocks.

"Why the hell doesn't he kill himself and be done with it?" Zooey wonders of the absent Buddy. (That Buddy Glass is putting this sentence in Zooey's mouth didn't hit me until two readings later, in my junior year of college. I noted the additional complexity in blue.) I trusted Zooey because he was angry. "I'm a twenty-five-year-old freak and she's a twenty-year-old freak, and both those bastards are responsible."

That was where I always stopped underlining. I never marked the last line of the scene, when Zooey makes fun of his mother's pitch-perfect exit ("In the old radio days, when you were all little and all, you all used to be so—smart and happy and—just *lovely*. Morning, noon, and night."), but softly, so that "his voice wouldn't really reach her down the hall."

It did not occur to me until after I had graduated from college that Salinger was entirely serious about the last third of the book, or that *Franny and Zooey* was intended as something other than a novel. I had always wondered about the little books that Franny carried in her purse, *The Way of a Pilgrim* and *The Pilgrim Continues His Way*. Her interest in the religious practice of a thirty-three-year-old Russian peasant with a withered arm who repeats the prayer "Lord Jesus Christ, have mercy on me" until it enters the rhythm of his heart always seemed to me like a precious symptom to which the author had devoted perhaps a little too much attention. What I realized, lying in bed in the basement, was that *Franny and Zooey* and *The Way of a Pilgrim* were similar, if not the same book. They were answers to the question of how to live.

The question interested me because I was twenty-three years old and living in my parents' basement in West Orange, New Jersey, along with the family dog, an unwashed poodle. Before that, I had been living in Manhattan, in a five-room apartment on East Fourteenth Street between Second and Third Avenues that I shared with five people between the ages of twenty-four and thirty-two. I paid $320 a month for a room with three doors and no windows. It was hot in the winter. The summer was worse. People wandered in and out. The building next door was a residence for the deaf, and at night its tenants would bring their Dominican boyfriends to our stairwell, lean up against the wall, spread their legs, open their mouths, and roll their eyes toward heaven without making a sound. Everyone I knew wore leather jackets and took drugs. Two of my roommates were heroin addicts. I was afraid to put a needle into my arm. Over time, I became afraid of the way I was living.

When I moved back home, I stopped taking drugs, which made me angrier than I had been before. I was also scared. In the book, Bessie Glass wanted to send Franny to an analyst, like Philly Byrnes.

"Philly *Byrnes*," Zooey answered. "Philly Byrnes is a poor little impotent sweaty guy past *forty* who's been sleeping for years with a rosary and a copy of *Variety* under his pillow." That wasn't me either. If there was someone out there with "any crazy, mysterious *grat*itude for his insight and intelligence," it wasn't any psychiatrist I knew. And it wasn't J. D. Salinger either. I was looking for answers, and the notes I made toward the end of the book at age twenty-four quiver with sardonic disappointment. "'Nancy Drew and the Hidden Staircase' lay on top of 'Fear and Trembling.'" That was Salinger's own line. But it seemed like a better description of the weakness of *Franny and Zooey* than anything I could invent on my own. I noticed that Franny is described as "a first-class beauty," and I found the description cheap. I marked Zooey's line to Franny: "How in *hell* are you going to recognize a legitimate holy man when you see one if you don't even know a cup of consecrated chicken soup when it's right in front of your nose?" In the margin I suggested that Starbucks could use this motto on a new line of greeting cards, to be sold at the cash register for a dollar apiece.

And those were the last words I wrote in my copy of *Franny and Zooey*. The affair had gone cold.

Reading the book again, for the first time as a writer, I was amazed by how many perfect moments there are, by how rich and funny and wise it is, by how much and how little I understood, and by the fact that the entire book is only two hundred pages long. I still love the bathroom scene the best. But I also love the end of the book, particularly the moment when Franny announces that she wants to talk to Seymour, the moment of pure emotion that the book has been building toward for almost the entire two hundred pages, and that Salinger, Buddy, and Zooey answer by looking out the window and seeing a little girl in a red tam, with her dachshund wandering on the sidewalk nearby. It's not Seymour exactly. It's the little girl from the airplane, or someone like her, a vision of sustaining innocence that will carry us through the harder part of the lesson, Seymour's Fat Lady, for whose sake Zooey Glass once polished his shoes every night before appearing on the radio. She had thick legs, very veiny, and her radio was always going full blast. She had cancer.

"There isn't anyone out there who isn't Seymour's Fat Lady," Zooey says. The Fat Lady is Christ. Or forgiveness. There was a time when this sentence didn't make sense, or didn't convince me to underline the words or put a check mark or a star in the margin. I'm not saying that the line is unsentimental. There may be higher peaks of wisdom to climb. Still, in the interests of full disclosure, it seems only fair to relate that after I closed the book, I opened it again, got out my fancy new disposable fountain pen, and added a black check mark to the author's italics. I am still grateful for this book. That is what I mean to say.

Relics of Saint Katherine

The *Journal*, *Letters*, and *Stories* of Katherine Mansfield

atherine Mansfield might have been for me, as she probably is for most readers, one of the usual suspects rounded up in the anthologies, represented by her "perfect" short story, "The Garden Party." She might have surfaced again in biographies of her more celebrated friends—Virginia Woolf, who saw her as a rival, and D. H. Lawrence, who used her as the model for Gudrun in *Women in Love*. And then she might have receded into that twilight where minor writers refuse to be extinguished entirely, trailing clouds of her "exquisite" sensibility, the unfulfilled promise of her talent excused by her early death.

Mansfield might have been no more than a filmy background figure had I come to her through her fiction. But I read her *Journal* and *Letters* first, documents pulsing with her ardent confusion of art and life, matters I was just beginning to scramble up myself. "I want to *work*," she confided to her journal,

> . . . so to live that I work with my hands and my feeling and
> my brain. I want a garden, a small house, grass, animals,
> books, pictures, music. And out of this, the expression of this,
> I want to be writing. (Though I may write about cabmen.
> That's no matter.) But warm, eager, living life—to be rooted in
> life—to learn, to desire to know, to feel, to think, to act. That
> is what I want.

She articulated for me what it was to want to *be* a writer—
and against heavy odds.

But even the autobiographical intimacy of those forms—
journals and letters—doesn't explain the fascination for
Mansfield that developed in my teens and persisted into my
twenties. The word "fascination" hardly states the case. For
years—in college and graduate school and beyond, through
dumb jobs and frequent moves from one crummy apartment
to another as I too tried "to be a writer"—home was where I
hammered a nail and hung my photograph of Mansfield's
hieratic, consumptive face. My shrine, my saint.

I read everybody with fierce appetite during those years—
Whitman, Woolf, Lawrence, poets beyond count. But I didn't
just *read* Mansfield. I stalked her. I chased down primary
sources, secondary sources, tracking any shred of memory or
gossip. When I learned from Frieda Lawrence's memoir that,
during the period when they had lived next door to each
other in Cornwall, Mansfield had introduced her to Cuticura
soap, I was off to Walgreens, dazzled to find that in 1968 it
was still possible to buy the assertive clove-scented bar. A relic.

I learned from one of Mansfield's biographers (for a
supposedly minor writer, she had quite a few) that she liked

to keep "low bowls of bright flowers" on her writing table: I affected the same. She favored little jackets of "lovely colours and soft velvet materials": soon my style as well, though my latter-day velvets draped over jeans. Mine was the moist devotion of a cultist, not the frank pleasure of a reader.

Of course I also read the short stories. I approved the transparency of Mansfield's prose, the click of her snapshot scenes, her pitch-perfect ear for a volley of dialogue, her descriptive delight in the world. The voice in my favorite stories ("Prelude," "At the Bay") combined a cool authority with an unspoken, and therefore all the more convincing, heartache for her lost New Zealand. I knew that her Wellington had hardly been cherished at the time. Like me in St. Paul, she knew she was a provincial, and she longed to escape—and she did, to London in 1908, before she was twenty. But successful nostalgia is bred of regret, and Katherine Mansfield was a great regretter. After her relatively brief wild-thing period, illness turned her into a pondering, sometimes frantic, invalid. Her gleeful escape was twisted into lonely exile.

Her fiction had a more aloof voice, of course, than the urgent *Journal* and *Letters*, but this too was evidence of her particular genius: the ability both to bare her soul and to write works of detached authority. She exposed the membrane between self and work, the porous fiber that transformed a raw girlish ambition and overheated poeticism into the remorseless assurance of fiction.

Why were there no novels? I wondered briefly, but even this lack turned into virtue: Mansfield was a miniaturist, not

a big-sweep writer, and all the finer for that, a noticer of moments and gestures, a tender of oblique details. She fretted
about this: "Don't I live in *glimpses only*?" she wrote in a letter. But she also understood that her idea of a story's form
was genuinely new, *"pure risk,"* as she said, moving not by
plot but by impression and association, episodes beaded on a
brief string of time. Her vision was essentially poetic, not
narrative, and this enlivened her voice and, for me, her appeal. Her "glimpses" gave her work—the stories as well as
the letters—a striking immediacy. For all her intensity, she
was not a fainter and swooner. She was modern and proud of
it. Her humor was mordant, even unkind. Her lyricism had a
squeeze of lemon.

Mansfield suffered—this too was important to me. She
died at thirty-four after enduring years of tuberculosis. Her
youthful death hovered everywhere, even in her most rhapsodic flights. No wonder there were no novels. But there was
nothing self-destructive about her: her tubercular lungs were
bursting to live, live. My saint might die, but extinguish herself? Never. Would Chekhov have killed himself? And Chekhov,
I learned from the critics (including Mansfield's husband and
arch promoter, John Middleton Murry), was the writer she
most resembled.

In fact, it seems to me now that she more truly resembled
Jean Rhys (Mansfield nailed the "woman alone" theme before Rhys got to it). Even more fundamentally, Colette was
her kin. Like Colette, Mansfield had her youthful cabaret period, complete with club performances and lesbian flirta-
tions, and though she wrote of the first generation of urban

"free" women, her signature was her sensuous evocations of nature. She wrote from her beloved Côte d'Azur:

> After lunch today, we had a sudden tremendous thunderstorm, the drops of rain were as big as marguerite daisies—the whole sky was violet. I went out the very moment it was over—the sky was all glittering with broken light—the sun a huge splash of silver. The drops were like silver fishes hanging from the tree.

Had she lived, she might very likely have become an English Colette, an earthier mother-of-us-all than Virginia Woolf.

Virginia Woolf might write to her sister, in an initial assessment of Mansfield, that she found her "cheap and hard . . . unscrupulous." But Mansfield had the keener eye for character, writing to Ottoline Morrell after this first meeting that she sensed in Woolf "the strange trembling, glinting quality of her mind. . . . She seemed to me to be one of those Dostoevsky women whose 'innocence' has been hurt."

The *Journal* and the *Letters* were suffused with consumptive ecstasy. She saw this in Lawrence: "I recognized his smile—just the least shade too bright . . . his air of being a touch more vividly alive than other people—the gleam . . ." Her "work," as she wrote in the *Journal*, became a kind of parallel universe, spiritualized, even sacralized, as the clock ran out. She spoke severely of "sinning against art." This too I revered: the religion of art.

Keats (dead at twenty-five, also of TB) was *her* saint. She wrote of him in her journal as of a colleague. Like her, he was a hero-worshiper: he lugged around a portrait of

Shakespeare wherever he lived. I perceived in—or created from—this relationship a lineage that lifted Mansfield out of the low-rent housing where she lodged in the anthologists' rented rooms. Boldly (if privately) I attached her to the great Romantic dynasty, as configured expressly by and for me: Shakespeare → Keats → Mansfield. I dragooned her into the firmament.

And who was going to stop me? It was the early 1970s, and we were supposed to be "discovering" women writers, wedging them into the literary canon any which way. Yet it is strange that I fastened on Mansfield. Virginia Woolf, whose novels I read at the time and admired, did not compel me to buy her brand of face soap. Mansfield was my girl. But then, I didn't "discover" her. She had been willed to me.

I must have been about seventeen when Doris Derman turned to me in her majestic old apartment off Summit Avenue in St. Paul and said in response to something I had said and have now entirely forgotten, "That is the sort of observation Katherine Mansfield made."

I had never heard of Katherine Mansfield. For a moment I thought Doris was referring to a friend of hers. In any case, Doris Derman, worldly mother of my first boyfriend, was willing to make the introduction. "You may have these," she said, and walked over to her ceiling-high bookcase (itself an essential prop of the life I hoped to enter: the life of the mind) and handed me two books, one bound in faded orange linen with a yet-more-faded green spine, the other in a sad blue with dull silver lettering. The orange, its title stamped in worn gold, was the *Letters*; the blue was the *Journal*.

It is hard to convey how stunned I was to realize that such personal writings had been *published*. Stories, novels, poems—these were the stuff of books, weren't they? But letters, diaries—I wrote them myself; I never imagined they could be "literature."

Doris Derman was the first person, aside from teachers, I heard speak with authority about books and writers. But her authority was different; she spoke not from a height but from within the precinct of the initiated. She had opinions, and they were based on nothing but her own taste and whim. This was unheard of in my convent-school world of hierarchy and certainty, where references to authority were . . . authoritative.

Living in the same neighborhood, in the same parish (as Catholic St. Paul referenced all civic boundaries), Doris knew my family, knew who I was and from whence I came. But we had never met until her son brought me home. He artlessly confessed to me that his mother had told him before this meeting, "Beware of a girl whose family believes the world is no bigger than Linwood Avenue between Lexington and Oxford." Our block.

I was neither hurt nor insulted by this tart dismissal, which, of course, I was not intended to hear. In fact, I approved. It confirmed my own readiness to dismiss St. Paul, which squashed me far more (I later thought) than Katherine Mansfield's stodgy Wellington had squashed her. But more than that: I was subtly thrilled that Doris had captured us, had summed us up—had written us, in effect. My family did not talk this way, did not think this way. The hauteur necessary to make such a remark, the aerial aloofness from, well, from Linwood between Lexington and Oxford, would have given my family nosebleeds. Doris's cool ability to consign us to the higher world of description—to fiction, really—won me even before I met her.

I understood that Doris had once "written." There was the definite sense that as someone who *had written*, she was in possession of talent, vast sums she held prudently in ethereal escrow. She was a good ten years older than the other mothers in the parish, and dyed her hair a blatant, unapologetic blond. She had no interest in school functions. She let her husband handle the grocery shopping and the driving and the dealings with nuns and teachers. He was a gentle man who seemed conscripted to serve her, nervously asking—as he handed her a drink he had mixed in the kitchen while she sat in the shadowy living room, reading—whether she felt all right. Though her husband was Catholic and of course her son was too, she was alluringly non-Catholic. In fact, it appeared she was not religious at all, perhaps an agnostic.

This was all good, good news.

I can't think of Katherine Mansfield without conjuring Doris Derman—not because she entrusted her books to me and set me on the particular literary path (favoring clarity and immediacy, the bittersweet but fundamentally comic point of view) that I still think of as the high road. Not even because she introduced me to the "personal voice" in literature when she handed me Mansfield's *Journal* and *Letters*, thus opening the door to memoir and the essay, forms I came to prize and practice. It's simply that, over the years, her passion for Mansfield has become more eloquent to me than my own strenuous teen-idol feelings.

Doris was a teenager when Mansfield died in 1923. She belonged to the generation that had just inherited the short skirts and bold bobbed haircuts that Mansfield, for one, made the daring symbol of the new woman. Doris saw Mansfield as a tantalizing bohemian big sister. She'd been up to no good, and look what happened: sick, alone, exiled, dead. Her slim "oeuvre" was dwarfed by the journals and the passionate correspondence, in which she alternately bemoaned her fate and shored up her courage and ever-dimming hopes with crystalline descriptions of the world about her. They are among the great letters in English literature, fairly compared to the letters of Keats.

Doris pondered all sides of the story, the glory of the bold escape from the provinces, the sexual high jinks, the brilliant lyric sensibility, the desperate final mysticism. The circumstances of Mansfield's death—a final massive hemorrhage at the Gurdjieff community near Fontainebleau, where she had gone to "purify" herself—bespoke both the barely grasped independence of the "new woman" and the dismal fate that awaited her for stepping outside the assigned circle of safety. It was what a later generation of women would call a liberated life. And you got hammered for it. Doris's fascination with Mansfield had to do with what she revealed about the catastrophic results of attempting to be free. Better to "have written" briefly, sometime in the past, better to sock your talent safely away. Better to stay high in the shadowy apartment on Summit Avenue, keep your hair glamour-bright, accept another drink from your hovering husband.

Mansfield was the doomed artist for Doris's generation. Make that the doomed woman artist: the exemplary figure who combined talent, youth, beauty, drive, and early death. Virginia Woolf, who committed suicide at fifty-nine, lived too long to be this kind of figure. The doomed artist must be extinguished before endeavor has fully transmitted itself into achievement. Death is the massive gilt frame that pulls the eye away from the work to the life. But that's the point: with certain writers it is impossible (and for Doris, undesirable) to separate the two. Doris was mesmerized not by the fire of Mansfield's talent but by the extinguished flame, the burnt wick.

Mansfield was her generation's version of Sylvia Plath. Or, to put it in the proper chronology, Plath was my generation's version—after another world war and much else (including the development of drugs to cure TB)—of Mansfield. Plath's suicide was, of course, the opposite of Mansfield's frantic dash—from French seaside to Swiss alpine chalet, from doctors to quacks and finally to a proto–New Age guru—to save herself. But like Mansfield's, Plath's talent and achievement were genuine. Their work would still count even if their lives had not been tragic. Without their early deaths, however, they would not have become exemplary— or cautionary—figures for the women who studied them so fervently.

In Mansfield, Doris Derman chose a woman on whom the fates descended, but whose pact with life itself not only remained unbroken but was cranked up to an almost excruciating pitch of desire and attachment. In Plath, my generation chose a model of brilliant sourness, a woman whose fury was finally directed at life itself, not at its cruel refusal to admit her and sustain her. Our choice of a suicide may be a gloomy commentary on my generation. But even if Plath was exemplary because she represented what we wished to avoid becoming, she was still the lost woman writer who came to haunt us, as Mansfield haunted Doris Derman. There was this difference, though: Doris, I think, felt companioned by Mansfield. She was, in spite of everything, a benign ghost.

Like Plath's, Mansfield's gifts were augmented by a journal, a voluminous correspondence, and a literary husband-editor. Mansfield's cool talent and her desperado life were indelibly bonded, if they had not been before, by John Middleton Murry's publication of the *Journal* in 1927, just four years after her death. The *Letters* followed swiftly in 1928. Although Mansfield knew a measure of literary, if not truly popular, fame in her lifetime, her appeal really hit its international stride as a result of Murry's decision to fashion her personal writing into books that allowed her to take, as he gushingly said, "her rightful place as the most wonderful writer and most beautiful spirit of our time."

In other words, as a disgusted friend remarked at the time, Murry was "boiling Katherine's bones to make soup."

Doris did not see it this way—and of course, neither did I. We believed in books. We spoke of them as of people whose integrity was above reproach, not objects fashioned and formed. We approved, even revered, the final rhapsodic line of the *Journal*: *"All is well."* We took the italics to heart, as if they conveyed a final triumphant testament. *All is well.*

Ah! Doris and I said, bowing our heads before the courageous farewell of our heroine. Ah!

Now, all these years later, I have come with two new friends, an Englishwoman and her Danish husband, to Bandol: Mansfield's Bandol, as I think of it, a quiet Mediterranean fishing village (in her day), a gleaming tourist town (in ours). I've been given an apartment for four months in a nearby town, as part of a writing fellowship—the sort of improbable postmodern perk that would have astonished Mansfield in her fruitless search for a safety net.

This day trip to Bandol is an unabashed pilgrimage, though my days as a cultist are over. Here, during separate visits, Mansfield wrote "Prelude" and "Bliss" (which I have just reread and have urged on my friends, glad the stories still seem fresh, glad to spread the word, as Doris once passed it to me). I have also reread some of the letters. But their magic has gone dark now. Gone, the old thrill of exalted sensibility, the breathless lyric acuity. Gone, the romantic scrim that saved me from seeing what it was all about: utter terror of the death bearing down on her.

We are looking for the place where Mansfield wrote "Bliss," the Hôtel Beau-Rivage, a name so evocative it sounds like a hotel in a story rather than a hotel where a story was written. It is a beautiful day, still winter, as people here insist, though as a Minnesotan I know that this is foolishness, that we are deep into spring, trees blossoming, tables set out for lunch, sailboats groaning companionably in their slips.

We have one of those lunches they write about in magazines. It is timeless and winey. There is crème caramel quivering under its burnt sugar in a fluted glass dish, and little cups of bitter coffee to set you straight at the end of the meal.

Then we walk up the street to the hotel, a great peachy Belle Epoque business, the grounds parklike and gracious. A very small old man is pruning, with shears far too big for him, an immense wisteria vine that covers an entire wall. The vine's main branch, espaliered against the stone wall, is as thick as a tree. The scent is overpowering.

The old man smiles at my request—he has heard this before—and silently leads us through the grounds to the hotel entrance, where we are handed over to a likewise diminutive old woman, either his mate or his colleague. She points to the plaque mounted in the vestibule. In French it says: "Three hours ago I finished my story 'Bliss.' Thank God I had great happiness in the writing of it."

The small woman nods as the old man did, ready to accommodate: yes, I may go up and see The Room. So up the little *ascenseur* we go, the little woman, Susan, Steffen, and I. Up to the top (third) floor—and there it is, the door open (all the doors of all the rooms are open, waiting for their nonexistent occupants). It's now a double room, as it had not been when Mansfield stayed here in 1918. Appliances are lined up along one wall to make a kitchenette. It is not exactly "seedy," not even "tacky," just honestly, seriously worn. The place was probably lovely in its day, but it looks as if it was redone in the miserable 1950s and left to pickle in its unhealthy browns and beiges, its sickish greens. Oddly, the very cheapness of the veneers, the "modern" furniture sighing with shabbiness—all of it enshrines the life of hired rooms and not much money: her life.

The little woman nods—I may step out through the double French doors onto the balcony. I am in the air, looking out—as she must have looked when she rose from her desk, after her three hours of "happiness in the writing"—to the same thrilling sea (more boats, more people, more everything now, but the same blue, the same exalted height). "She took the best room," the tiny old woman murmurs, as if to say we all know that Katherine would of course take the best.

My new friend Susan, who has not yet read Mansfield, is wiping away tears. "Thank goodness she had happiness in the writing," she says. "She had so little happiness."

"Katherine has been dead a week," Virginia Woolf wrote in her diary after the news came from France:

> At that one feels—what? A shock of relief?—a rival the less? Then confusion at feeling so little—then, gradually, blankness & disappointment; then a depression which I could not rouse myself from all that day. When I began to write, it seemed to me there was no point in writing. Katherine wont read it.

Katherine's my rival no longer. . . . Still there are things about
writing I think of & want to tell Katherine. And I was jealous
of her writing—the only writing I have ever been jealous of.

It was sometime in the late 1980s that I read this rawly
honest passage. Woolf's diaries were being published, the
biographies were coming thick and fast. There was more about
Mansfield as well. It turned out, according to a carefully
sleuthed biography by Claire Tomalin, that although
Mansfield had indeed died of tuberculosis, it was undiag-
nosed gonorrhea, contracted during her first year of "freedom," that had weakened her and left her fatally vulnerable.

So much for freedom. Even the *Journal's* *"All is well"* finale
proved to be a bit of stagecraft—John Middleton Murry's.
He had not simply "edited" the *Journal*; he had orchestrated
it, piecing bits together to form a narrative that ended with
this apparent triumph of the spirit.

But I could not tell this to Doris. She was long gone by the
time I read the post-cult biographies. My mother, still living
in the neighborhood, had reported that people first noticed
that the milkman (the milkman!) was showing up later and
later on his rounds. Drinking at the Dermans, was the word.
Doris was dead drunk at 10:00 a.m., according to the woman
at the drugstore. Also: seen wandering on Grand Avenue,
alarming blond hair in disarray, wearing bathroom slippers
in the snow.

Then, not seen at all, spending all her time in the dark,
the blinds pulled, not even sobering up when her husband
came home, the children grown up and well out of it by now.

Finally, sprawled on the bathroom floor, "found" by her husband when he came home from work downtown.

We had read the last line of the *Journal* as a message to us, almost a directive. *All was well.* Doris and I stayed with Mansfield to the end, past the little pleasures of tea at the Villa Isola Bella in lemon-sunny Menton, where she wrote some of her best late stories. We followed her to the thin air of Sierre, high in the Alps, past her furious disappointment in Murry. Doris had made short work of him. "Obviously a drip," she said. We stayed with Katherine (as we called her) right to the moment she entered the weird community at Fontainebleau and died her gasping, operatic death after running up a flight of steps. "She was so happy," Doris had told me. It was as if she were there. "She forgot to be careful."

Still, *all was well.* Katherine had said so. Doris never had reason to disbelieve her testimony. Or maybe Doris kept to herself just how well she thought everything really was. Maybe she didn't wish to disillusion me; maybe she wanted to pass along the literary torch, burning with a "too bright" gleam but, all the same, shedding the only light that mattered to us.

My mother saw it more simply. "Doris was a fine woman," she said, as if someone had suggested otherwise. She did not like the gossip about the milkman. "She was a lady. She had talent." Then she paused, searching for what she really meant, what between us was highest praise: "She was a serious reader."

Love's Wound, Love's Salve

Pan, by Knut Hamsun

hen I was growing up in Michigan, my mother was the great reader in my family, and my father, though deeply creative in his professional life, did not read at all. I worked out a big part of my Oedipal conflict, if that's what it was, by becoming a reader myself. I found my way to my mother by heeding her signals; I turned to the authors she loved—at least those I could read—and soaked up whatever approval came my way. I imagined I saw my father scowling in the background.

My mother not only read—daily and with steady fixation—but also spoke with open reverence about writers, relishing the sound of their names and book titles and the bits of lore she gleaned from the biographies she devoured. I knew about Hemingway and Hadley, Isak Dinesen and her coffee plantation, Steinbeck and his dog Charley, long before I'd read any of these writers myself. All the news, however, came to me in the home language, Latvian, so that my own first encounters with my mother's authors—Wolfe, Maugham, London, and others—always carried a tinge of strangeness laid over the base of familiarity.

The effect of her devotion and the immersions it compelled—apart from the sheer pleasure of time spent in a vivid elsewhere—was to impress on me the idea that there was nothing finer, nothing worthier, than reading, except, of course, the writing that made reading possible.

While my mother loved a great many books and writers, she reserved a special reverence—so it seemed to me—for a handful of authors from her youth in Riga, especially those she had first read in her own early years as part of a series called Lielie Ziemeļnieki (Great Northerners), all issued, as she described them to me many times, in handsome uniform bindings: Sigrid Undset, Selma Lagerlöf, but above all others, Knut Hamsun, his *Hunger*, *Mysteries*, *Victoria*, and *Pan*, those works of desperate lyrical romanticism.

I offer this as prologue to help explain why my encounter in late adolescence with *Pan*—to my mind still one of the most heart-wrenching novels ever written—should have seemed so intense, so intended. I was not just reading a novel; I was also somehow making inroads on what I imagined was my mother's secret inner terrain. I was finding a connection to a world that predated me; in the process, I could feel myself putting down the first frail roots of my own private life.

People sometimes speak of those rare charged encounters between reader and book when ready tinder is touched by the flame point of a particular vision. The image describes something of my original experience with this most harrowing of Hamsun's early works. For *Pan*, published when its author was still in his thirties, is nothing if not the most numbingly pure distillation of a young heart's passion, of raw emotion unchecked by the rationalizations and deferrals that experience teaches.

As it happens, I read this little novel in the depths of my own most lovelorn summer. I was sixteen and abjectly in love with K. Tall, blond, dreamily pretty, K. was two classes behind me, very nearly still a girl, though she possessed the disconcerting poise you sometimes find in the truly beautiful, poise that can almost seem like submission to an unsolicited gift.

I hid my passion. I had to, for it would have chased K. away, and I could not imagine not being able to be near her. K.—this was very clear—saw herself as my friend, my companion in reverie, a fellow seeker. On summer nights, after a long day of working in a candy warehouse, I would drive to the Cranbrook School, where her father was the dean of students, and she and I would walk around the grounds, circling the lake in the growing twilight, me at every second aware of the nearness of her bare shoulder, the sway of her long hair, the little modulations of tone when she laughed at my jokes. I dreamed of my fingers brushing that skin, but I did not dare the slightest inclination in her direction. Later, though, driving home down Lone Pine Road, windows open to the night, or lying on my back in my stark and stuffy little room, I felt I would break apart if something did not happen soon.

———

It was in this state that I first read—gulped down—
Hamsun's novel and found myself transported into a sadness
from which it seemed there could be no return, that felt, suddenly, like my first earned wisdom, confirmation of the fact
that life touched by the genius of love was ultimately not to
be endured.

Hamsun opens with the account—seemingly innocent,
contemplative, transparent—of one Lieutenant Glahn, who
would have us believe he is passing the time setting down a
few recollected episodes from a summer that has already
taken on the character of a dream:

> These last few days I have thought and thought of the Nordland
> summer's endless day. I sit here and think of it, and of a hut I
> lived in, and of the forest behind the hut; and I have taken to
> writing about it, just for my own amusement and to while away
> the time. Time drags; it does not pass as quickly as I should like,
> although I have no cares and lead the gayest of lives. I am per-
> fectly content with everything, and thirty is no great age. A
> few days ago I received a couple of bird's feathers from far
> away, from one who need not have sent them; just two green
> feathers folded in a sheet of paper with a coronet on it and fas-
> tened with a seal. It amused me to see two so fiendishly green
> feathers. Otherwise there is nothing to trouble me except a
> touch of arthritis now and then in my left foot, the result of an
> old shot wound that healed up long ago.
>
> I remember that time went much faster two years ago, in-
> comparably faster than now; the summer was gone before I re-
> alised it. It was two years ago, in 1855—I want to write about
> it to amuse myself—that something happened to me: or else I
> dreamt it.

Glahn would have us believe that he is a man at peace, but even an unsophisticated reader—such as I surely was in that long-ago summer of 1968—must grasp that these are the bravely bitter posturings of a man looking to master his pain. Phrases like "for my own amusement" and "although I have no cares" are, we know, standard-issue denials; but just in case we don't pick this up, there is the protruding giveaway "Otherwise there is nothing to trouble me," confirming, lest we doubt it, that the receipt of the two green feathers was not an unalloyed pleasure. The beauty and power of *Pan* lies in how completely the gradually revealed emotional lacerations come to contradict Glahn's adopted pose.

The outer contour of Glahn's summer, the slight stuff of plot, is easily sketched in. Glahn is, by temperament, one of life's great romantic solitaries. Taking a break from the larger world, living in a forest hut near a small Norwegian trading village, he passes his summer alone, with only his beloved dog, Aesop, for company. When he is hungry, he hunts. Otherwise, he whiles away the endless hours daydreaming in his hut or wandering about in the forest, communing with nature in fugues of such pantheistic intensity that it seems at times he will simply merge with the great green Other: "Over by the edge of the forest there is fern and monk's hood, the heather is in bloom and I love its small flowers. I thank God for every heather flower I have ever seen; they have been like tiny roses on my path and I weep for love of them."

It cannot last, this perfect peace, this ecstatic natural concord. Into Eden comes Eve, in the form of Edvarda, the young daughter of Herr Mack, owner of the village trading post. She appears at Glahn's hut one day in the company of the stolidly pretentious man called simply the Doctor. He and Edvarda have been out walking and have decided to pay a call on Glahn.

The three talk awkwardly, moving from subject to subject, and only when the visitors have left are we allowed to grasp the intense fixity with which Glahn has been regarding Edvarda: "Suddenly I saw before me her brown face and brown neck. She had tied her apron low on her hips to accentuate the length of her body, as was fashionable. Her thumb had a chaste and girlish look about it that touched me; and the few wrinkles on her knuckles were full of kindliness. She had a generous mouth, and her lips were red." This, we realize, is not the fruit of idle observation, but something else. These details have been gathered by the eye of the avid soul, the same eye that casts abroad in the forest for intimations of our higher connectedness.

The attraction proves to be mutual, whereupon, in keeping with the ancient principle of romantic magnetism, operative whenever two people think only of each other, Glahn and Edvarda are soon encountering one another everywhere—on the forest paths, down in the village. Here is the pure intoxication of young love, and if the particulars vary slightly across the surface, deep down they are subject to the delicious lifts and plunges of the universal erotic dance:

"You are happy to-day, you are singing," she says, and her eyes sparkle.

"Yes, I am happy," I answer. "You have a smudge of something on your shoulder there, it's dust, from the road perhaps. I want to kiss it—no, please, let me kiss it! Everything about you arouses tenderness in me, I am quite distracted by you. I didn't sleep last night."

And that was true; for more than one night I had lain sleepless.

Edvarda takes the first deeper initiative. She comes to Glahn's hut and, declaring her full passion, stays the night and plants the barb of the hook so that it will never be extricated.

The congruence, the easy blending of their affections is soon—who knows why—pushed into a terrible discontinuity. Glahn catches the first intimation: "Sometimes there would be a night when Edvarda stayed away; once she stayed away for two nights. Two nights. There was nothing wrong, and yet I had the feeling that my happiness had passed its peak." Whether this is an illustration of what Proust called "the intermittencies of love"—as if affection were a flame that must rise and fall—or simply something perverse in the deep down nature of things, some fateful coupling of eros and sadism, the idyll of Glahn and Edvarda changes track almost as soon as it has begun.

Now follows the mad Lawrentian combat of the wills. Edvarda pulls away; Glahn suffers, sulks, practices his own stratagems of indifference. Then, just when he is strengthening toward a new resolve, ready to cut her loose, Edvarda flashes the ray of her vulnerable sweetness, and Glahn is drawn back into the circuit of wanting and hoping.

Sitting near Glahn on a group outing to a nearby island, Edvarda admires the beautiful feathers he uses for tying flies. Glahn promptly gives her two. "Please take them," he says, "let them be a memento." But later, when they are returning in a rowboat together, Glahn seizes Edvarda's shoe and flings it far out over the water. He does not begin to understand his own impulse. The air between them is crackling with disturbance.

So things continue for a time—sightings, meetings, rebuffs, spasms of searing jealousy whenever Glahn sees Edvarda giving her attention to another. The tension pushes them apart. Edvarda no longer comes to the hut at night. Glahn wanders about, disconsolate, but all obvious emotion is thrust below the waterline; he betrays none of his feelings when they chance to meet. As readers, however, we need no compass. We can reckon the state of his heart from his erratic actions, his distractedness, his willed affair with another village girl. Nothing avails this poor man. His erotic grief has no way to discharge itself, and as it builds, he is driven ever more irretrievably into himself.

Weeks then pass without encounter; summer is slowly winding down. As the time for Glahn's departure draws near, the pressure of his longing and frustration grows almost intolerable for the reader.

Then, just days before he must go, he unexpectedly meets Edvarda at the counter of the village store:

> I greeted her, and she looked up but did not answer. Then it occurred to me that I did not want to ask for bread while she was

there; I turned to the assistants and asked for powder and shot. While these were being weighed I kept my eye on her.

A grey dress, much too small for her, its buttonholes worn; her flat breast heaved desperately. How she had grown during the summer! Her brow was pensive, those strange arched eyebrows were set in her face like two riddles, all her movements had become more mature. I looked at her hands, the expression in her long, delicate fingers affected me powerfully and made me tremble.

On the day of his departure, almost as an afterthought—so he portrays it—Glahn decides he must say farewell to Edvarda. He finds her at home, sitting with a book. His news seems to startle her, though we pick up but the slightest hint:

"Glahn, are you going away? Now?"

"As soon as the ship comes." I seize her hand, both her hands, a senseless rapture takes possession of me and I burst out: "Edvarda!" and stare at her.

And in an instant she is cold, cold and defiant.

Edvarda can only say: "To think that you are leaving already!" A moment later she adds: "Who will come next year, I wonder?" Whereupon she seats herself with her book. The interview is over.

But no—suddenly, perversely, she rises to her feet again with a parting request.

"I should like something to remind me of you when you have gone," she said. "There was something I thought of asking you for, but perhaps it is too much. Will you give me Aesop?"

Without reflecting I answered "Yes."

Later, alone in his hut, Glahn agonizes over his decision:

> Why had she asked me to come and bring the dog myself? Did she want to talk to me, tell me something for the last time? I had nothing more to hope for. And how would she treat Aesop? Aesop, Aesop, she will torment you! Because of me she will whip you, caress you too perhaps, but certainly whip you in and out of season and utterly destroy you. . . .
>
> I called Aesop, patted him, put our two heads together and reached for my gun. He was already whining with pleasure, thinking we were going out hunting. Again I put our heads together, placed the muzzle of the gun against Aesop's neck and fired.
>
> I hired a man to carry Aesop's body to Edvarda.

So much for Glahn's coy disingenuousness: "It amused me to see two so fiendishly green feathers." Indeed. Has Nordic stoicism, the most indurate of all stoicisms, ever shown itself more starkly? Has the blade of unrequited love ever turned quite so painfully in its wound? When I read these words, I was in the grip, I then imagined, of my passion for my own Edvarda. K., so shy to begin with, would grow perceptibly more aloof whenever I brought myself the slightest bit closer to risking some admission. Now I understood; Hamsun had given me the hard news about love. And about life—for in the wake of such utter devastation it seemed there was little point in anything else. I took that sadness down into the center of my heartsick summer and incubated it there.

Pan concludes with a section called "Glahn's Death: A Paper from the Year 1861." Six years later, in other words.

The short section comes to us in the voice of a bitter comrade of Glahn's ("But Thomas Glahn had his faults, and I am not disposed to conceal them, since I hate him"), a man who first met the lieutenant two years earlier somewhere in India or Ceylon. The gist of the "paper"—a confession, or self-exoneration, of sorts—is that the mysterious and erratic Glahn, after befriending him, began to goad him systematically, setting up a situation in which the man would have no choice but to shoot him. One day when they were out hunting together he did just that:

> The court entered his name and the circumstances of his death in a stitched and bound register, and in that register is written that he is dead, I tell you, yes, and even that he was killed by a stray bullet.

How can we ever gauge the effects of a work like this on a susceptible young reader? I was shaken to the core. I was just sixteen; I had no wisdom to hold against this vision of hopelessness, no mitigating perspective. I had only the riot of my own emotions, the certainty that if K. would not recognize and greet my love, I would have nothing to get me through my life. The only thing that cut against my despair was my hope. K. and I were still seeing each other, walking and talking; she was still hearing out my thoughts and confidences. Somehow I would bring her to see who I was, how I loved her.

I never did. K. told me one day in late July that she was going away for a month with her family. I swallowed the sudden absence like some horrid emetic—I had no choice—

and I resolved to wait. While she was gone, I did everything I could to make myself into the person she would want to be with. I lost weight. I whittled my soul into something sharp and fierce. But when summer ended, when she returned, I had changed. I have no explanation for what happened. Time had worked its decisive will: I had miraculously moved away from wanting her. When, a few weeks later, someone else suddenly appeared in my life, I gave everything I had hoarded to her.

Still, I was not able to look at *Pan* for many years. It compressed so much of my pain, my longing, in its pages, and even the receding memory was a threat. My deepest unhappiness was secreted there. And I had the superstition that if I were to open the cover and glance at the words, I might somehow come unstitched. The book was put away. And when I went to college, moving my prize possessions, mainly books, from one place to another, I did not bring *Pan* with me.

Just a month ago, imagining myself ready to write about the novel, I bought a marked-up paperback and, in a spirit of edgy curiosity, began to read. I expected that I would prevail over the romanticism; that its mainspring—Glahn's brooding stoicism—would now strike me as forced; that his communings with nature would seem overheated. I was armed to the teeth.

And utterly powerless. For such is the power of a book, a memory, that it can in a flash outwit any structure or system we have raised against it. I had, yes, steeled myself against

Glahn, against the sorrow of his story, against his complete destruction by the passion that had erupted in his unguarded heart. I had not, however, braced against the encounter with myself, the sixteen-year-old who went at the world, at the dream of love, with such unscreened intensity. I read *Pan*, but the person I met on those woodland paths was my feverish younger self. I felt sorrow from the first sentence on, sorrow so sweet and piercing that it was hard to turn the pages. Worse, though—for sorrow recollected can bring a certain pleasure—was my self-reproach. As I read I indicted myself. I had, in stages, without ever planning it, traded off that raw nerved-up avidness. I'd had to, of course; it was inevitable. We do not survive the dream of love, not at that pitch. We build in our safeguards and protective reflexes. We give in to the repetitions, let them gradually tame the erratic element. We grow wise and find balance—or perish. Still, to encounter the stalking ghost of the self here, now, at midlife . . .

But no, I have found the rationale, the way to understand. Indeed, when it came to me, I felt a great rush of relief. "This is *not* the tragic truth of things." I actually said it out loud. I remember. I was walking along a scenic path in Bennington, Vermont, just two weeks ago, trying to make sense of this old business for the hundredth time in my life.

The thought formed itself so clearly. What Hamsun offers is not the final truth, because whatever it tells about love, it somehow leaves out the people who do the loving. *Pan* is the legend of desire feasting upon itself, struggling against itself, turning on itself to eradicate the unendurable pain, the source of all wanting. Glahn and Edvarda are just figures in the dance. They have nothing to hold up against the pulverizing momentum in their separate souls. They have, I saw it now, no . . . relationship. And realizing this saved me from the harshest effects of my sadness, allowed me to close the book up around the beautiful black feather I keep as a bookmark, allowed me my equanimity, which is now punctured, but not riddled, by secret doubts.

Whitman's Triumph

"Song of Myself," by Walt Whitman

n the Monday after the World Trade Center attack, I taught "Song of Myself" to my first-year-studies class in poetry (half literary survey, half workshop) at Sarah Lawrence. The class was the first group of freshmen I'd been put in charge of, and, nervous about facing people so young and expectant and free from dissimulation, I had planned the syllabus, in August, while vacationing in Vermont, with a minute and excessive rigidity: Whitman and Dickinson first, then a long leap back to Donne and Herbert, followed by a massive progression through Milton, Smart, Blake, Wordsworth's and Shelley's prose manifestos, Hardy and Hopkins, and then, in late November and early December, the blizzards of modernism—all of this buttressed by supplemental critical texts and contemporary poems that illustrated the persistence and continuity of theme, rhetoric, strategy. A muscle-bound course—but one that I was convinced would make my students, about whose respect

for the past glories of poetry I was dubious, love the art as
they never had before.

The syllabus I'd assembled in the Green Mountains during the summer had lost its specific density, and even a lot of
its meaning, by that Monday; but the imperative, at the college and across New York City, which begins a few miles to
the south, beyond Yonkers, was to get on with it, to affirm the
ordinariness of our existences and the privilege, until then
taken for granted, of the day-to-day business of working and
living and studying, which, among other things, the murder-
ers had sought to annihilate. I was as sedulous as anybody
about getting on with it. I went into my Monday class thinking that we had already lost the previous Thursday's session
to confusion and grief and talk that went nowhere, and that
we had to turn back to the demands of my schedule. The
dust from the collapse of the towers had been carried by the
prevailing winds to the South Brooklyn neighborhood, just
across the East River from Manhattan's financial district,
where I live. That Tuesday and Wednesday, the air had been
thick and infernal. There was an asbestos scare abroad. We
were told not to go out without masks. Dust that was once
the World Trade Center made the leaves of the plane trees
and the ginkgoes spectral; it tarnished the pavements and
covered the cars. All that week and into the next, I was
among the millions of people in the city ricocheting from
blank shock to incomprehension to grief to—this a liberation and a satisfaction, and the only energetic feeling most of
us could summon—defiance (though defiance of what, I
couldn't have said). From my roof, I'd seen the first tower

collapse, and had already heard one of the stories about people I knew who had died, but in keeping with this strange defiance—which seemed atavistic, which antedated thought, and which was hardwired into the organism itself—and though it seemed almost sacrilegious, the first thing I did when I got back to Brooklyn from my Thursday class was to take my car to the local car wash and clean the dust off.

My freshman class might have been feeling something of the same defiance. They didn't, in any case, take to "Song of Myself," and they let me know it. A couple of them tried, halfheartedly, to defend Whitman, but most thought that what they called his "egotism"—a character trait vivid to people their age—was unattractive. The events of the previous week—their first week of classes in their first semester at college, a time, in normal circumstances, of anticipation and adventure—had made them wary and self-contained. They were politely incredulous when I pointed out this line (in the 1855 version of the poem, which was the one we were using): "I am the man . . . . I suffered . . . . I was there." When I read the lines that follow soon after, lines that repeated quotation would make famous in subsequent weeks,

> *I am the mashed fireman with breastbone broken . . . . tumbling*
> *   walls buried me in their debris,*
> *Heat and smoke I inspired . . . . I heard the yelling shouts of my*
> *   comrades,*
> *I heard the distant click of their picks and shovels;*
> *They have cleared the beams away . . . . they tenderly lift me*
> *   forth.*

I lie in the night air in my red shirt . . . . the pervading hush is for
   my sake,
Painless after all I lie, exhausted but not so unhappy,
White and beautiful are the faces around me . . . . the heads are
   bared of their fire-caps,
The kneeling crowd fades with the light of the torches.

they said yes, he was empathetic and prescient, but returned to the question of his self-love. Wasn't this another one of its manifestations? they asked, with a sophistication about human motives that I found impressive (though, in this case, misplaced). I told them that the poem, untitled in the 1855 edition, was called "Walt Whitman" through successive editions of *Leaves of Grass* after 1856, until the comprehensive edition of 1881 (the one that was banned in Boston), when it came to be called by the name we know. Didn't such aplomb, so barefaced, so unashamed, actually subvert conventional ideas about egotism, and suggest that something else was at work? No, they said. A poet who would call a poem by his own name had some real problems. I told them about the Upanishads and the Oversoul. I talked about Whitman's fresh and original use of the English language, unequaled outside Shakespeare: "Blacksmiths with grimed and hairy chests environ the anvil"—that verb choice, so precise, visual, and unexpected; the wonderful play of the conjunct consonants; the clash as of metals between "environ" and "anvil"—and "Happiness . . . . which whoever hears me let him or her set out in search of this day," with its nested, overlapping relative clauses handled with speed and effortless athleticism. I told them that "Song of Myself," which seems so much like a natural object, a mountain range or a piece of driftwood, was, in fact, strictly Aristotelian, with a beginning, a middle, and an end; a turn in its curious plot (wherein a certain individual born on Long Island the same year as Herman Melville becomes the universe itself); and a moment of discovery, which occurs in and around the fireman passage. I drew their attention to the lines in "The Sleepers" in which the poet transforms himself into a woman and has a sexual encounter that concludes with the line "I feel the hot moisture yet that he left me."

"Can you believe that?" I asked. "'I feel the hot moisture yet that he left me'!"

"Yuck!" they replied.

My students weren't being obtuse or perverse. They were right to be skeptical. Under a lot of the circumstances of reading and rereading, there is something endlessly suspicious about Whitman; the endlessness of the suspicion is, in fact, one of the indications of his stature. The tremendous access of reality, the constant presence of incidental beauty, and the lines themselves, tense with meaning yet so relaxed, are never sufficient to protect us from the invasiveness of the all-or-nothing Whitman proposition. And his enthusiasms spring from, and bear the mark of, the choicer elements of the freakish era in which he lived: phrenology and P. T. Barnum; animal magnetism and hydropathy; harebrained schemes to invade Canada; manifest destiny; the Mexican War (of which Whitman was an egregious journalistic booster, and about which Grant, a sober political realist of great integrity, said, "For myself, I was bitterly opposed to the mea-

sure, and to this day regard the war, which resulted, as one of
the most unjust ever waged by a stronger against a weaker
nation"); ham actors; chautauquas; the Burnt-Out District;
the inexorable march to Fort Sumter. This is the frenzied atmosphere of which "Song of Myself" is the exuberant, ex-
haustive, and—except for rare clunkers like "You should
have been with us that day round the chowder-kettle"—perfect embodiment. Approached in the wrong mood, or from
the wrong angle, it can all seem a little too much.

But what angle was right? Sitting at the seminar table, I
sensed that I wasn't doing justice to this poem, which I had
read and marveled over since the age of sixteen, when, as a
freshman myself, in an introductory poetry course similar to
this one, I'd encountered it in the anthology we were assigned, *The Mentor Book of Major American Poets*, a book I
still have. The poem had never shaped my writing. On the
life I lived in the years after college, though, it had exerted a
powerful subterranean influence. The last time dust and ash
from a cataclysm had fallen on my car had been in May of
1980, when Mount Saint Helens had erupted. Temporarily
homeless, I was living in my 1970 Volkswagen bus (red, with
a gold hand-painted top), which I parked at night in a small,
long-abandoned drive-in theater, surrounded by the trees of
the Coast Range, in South Beach, on the central Oregon
coast. My life then had been one that Whitman not only
would have approved of but had practically invented: my oc-
cupation was Jeffersonian (I was a commercial salmon fish-

erman, though not an entirely effective one); my central ideas were pantheistic; my friends were "powerful uneducated persons"—Whitman's children of Adam. (Looking back now, I see the way I was living as almost comically Whitmanesque, though I was as convinced about what I was doing in those days as I've ever been.) I woke up that May morning to find a fine coat of gray dust, carried two hundred miles west by the weather and clotted a little in places because there had been an early-morning squall, covering my car. Mount Saint Helens had had its victims, too, though that dust, unlike this dust, had seemed to be one of the unambiguous blessings of nature.

I had, therefore, a small personal stake in the poem, in the appeal of its creed and the validity of its imperatives. How was I going to justify it to these skeptical children? A little confused, I let the discussion go on without me for a minute or two, feeling that slightly vertiginous panic which teachers at a loss for words feel. Then, in repudiation of the word "pantheism," which was bouncing around in my head and calling up images of the Pacific seen from Yaquina Head and of Yaquina Bay bristling with salmon boats (and flushed out, maybe, by the emotions of the past six days— emotions that, though they ranged from grief to rage, were suffused with a sense of powerlessness), I had an insight. I'd reread the Puritan divines from Edwards to Emerson over the past summer; I'd reread Justin Kaplan's biography of Whitman; I had picked, sometimes inattentively (there's a lot of dreck there), over the entire Whitman corpus. But something about the poem had escaped me—had, in fact,

until that moment, *always* escaped me. I took out the copy of
the Bible I'd brought to class in order to read, if we had time
to look at "Crossing Brooklyn Ferry" ("Flood-tide below me!
I see you face to face!"), Saint Paul's telling the church at
Corinth that now we see through a glass darkly but then we
will see face-to-face. I told my class that "Song of Myself"
was understood in the collective critical mind as a pantheistic poem, an ardent poem, a revolutionary poem, but that it
was actually a poem of the severest orthodoxy and hardness,
and coldness, even; that it was understood as a mystical poem,
an "Eastern" poem, a Vedantic poem, but that while many
things in it might justify such an interpretation, its structure, its inner body, its circulatory rhythms, suggested something else. Whitman was, I told my students, far closer to
Edwards than he was to Emerson (Emerson, for that matter,
was far closer to Edwards than he was to Emerson). For all
his empathy and his eroticism, for all his modernity and his
gee-whiz mastery of the vocabulary of nineteenth-century
popular science (the employment, for example, of the word
"oscillating" to describe the bodies of flying seagulls in
"Crossing Brooklyn Ferry"—how did he come up with that?),
Whitman was in the business of writing something admon-
itory and militant and ancient and Western. The text he was
expounding was this one:

> *Behold, I shew you a mystery; We shall not all sleep, but we shall
>   all be changed,*
> *In a moment, in the twinkling of an eye, at the last trump; for the
>   trumpet shall sound, and the dead shall be raised incorrupt-
>   ible, and we shall be changed.*

For this corruptible must put on incorruption, and this mortal
   must *put on immortality.*
So when this corruptible shall have put on incorruption, and this
   mortal shall have put on immortality, then shall be brought
   to pass the saying that is written, Death is swallowed up in
   victory.
O death, where is *thy sting? O grave, where* is *thy victory?*

The drama the poem enacted was the triumph over death.

To think, however accurately, that you've had a peak-in-Darien experience, that you've come across something so simple and inevitable it is presumptively true, can be pretty exhilarating. The class period ended on my suspended trumpet note, we broke up, and I walked away in the grip of a revelation. It was as if I had dreamed up the structure of the benzene ring or discovered the gravitational force. Of course. "Song of Myself" and "Crossing Brooklyn Ferry" (the 1856 *Paradiso*, with Manhattan as the city on the hill) were as allegorical as the *Divine Comedy*, and were as enmeshed in the same cosmic narrative, though now abstracted. "I stop some where waiting for you," Whitman says at the end of "Song of Myself," and there he was. The triumph over death. Almost a dozen people I knew who worked in the buildings had escaped; two I knew, who had been leading lives as ordinary as my own—lives that might just as well have been my own—hadn't. Their stories, and the stories of all those others, bouncing between the two absences in the skyline— back and forth, back and forth—gave the depression and grief an uncontainable energy. And always, when I thought I was back to myself, alone with myself, there were, available to automatic glances from many corners in my neighborhood, and from points along which I traveled, the sickening absences in the skyline.

I taught "Song of Myself" again that week. I went and talked about Whitman on Thursday evening, at the invitation, proffered months before, of Alice Quinn, *The New Yorker*'s poetry editor, to a class she teaches at Columbia. These were graduate students, and many were longtime residents of the city. They were somber and uninterested in disputes, and listened quietly when, after a half hour of preliminaries, I laid out my argument. I began with the fireman passage, lines 843 to 850 in the 1855 edition. Work your way around the strange terrain the poem has just traversed to arrive at this point, I told them. The border begins at these extraordinary lines (709–14):

> *Swift wind! Space! My Soul! Now I know it is true what I guessed at;*
> *What I guessed when I loafed on the grass,*
> *What I guessed while I lay alone in my bed . . . . and again as I walked the beach under the paling stars of the morning.*
>
> *My ties and ballasts leave me . . . . I travel . . . . I sail . . . . my elbows rest in the sea-gaps,*
> *I skirt the sierras . . . . my palms cover continents,*
> *I am afoot with my vision.*

Notice the psychic tension, amounting to what some might call insanity. A catalog follows. What he guessed at long ago in the poem, when he loafed on the grass, is that the "smallest sprout shows there is really no death," that "All goes onward and outward . . . . and nothing collapses, / And to die is different from what anyone supposed, and luckier." But something has happened between those assertions and this catalog, which is twin of the catalog that begins at line 257 ("The pure contralto sings in the organloft"), the magnificent aria of the human occupations. The earlier catalog was in the third person. This one is in the first person: "I am the hounded slave . . . Hell and despair are upon me"; "I visit the orchards of God and look at the spheric product" (spectacular, that "spheric product"); "I turn the bridegroom out of bed and stay with the bride myself." The first catalog was sunny and ideal, and melodic, as were the assertions of the good news of death. This one is Whitman's *Liebestod*, beginning in a derangement of the senses ("my elbows rest in the sea-gaps . . . my palms cover continents"), continuing in spasms of disintegrative energy, and culminating in episodes of destruction and violence—the fireman, "the fall of grenades through the rent roof," the massacre at Goliad. "It cannot fail," Whitman insists through the images of suffering and death that crowd around the last third of the poem. "To any one dying . . . . thither I speed and twist the knob of the door"; "O despairer . . . I dilate you with tremendous breath"; "The weakest and shallowest is deathless with me." Everywhere the verse is fragmentary, self-erasing; it "oscillates" wildly. The triumph over death leads to the again sunny and spacious assimilations ("And any man or woman shall stand cool and supercilious before a million universes") that end the poem.

I told the class that Whitman shows us who he really is here. Here—not in the doctrine of the poem but in the distribution of its energies, in the jagged, feverish expansions of the writing—he reveals himself not as the pantheist, the mystic, the sage, but as the Christian soldier setting out to harrow the underworld. Many people have pointed out the sea change in the poem, I said, but until now no one has guessed at what it means. Blissfully unaware of whether this last statement was true or not—I've always made sure to stay ignorant of the Whitman critical literature—I ended there, took some questions, thanked the assembled students, and went home. But I was filled with my idea for days, and didn't really begin to let it go until the bombing started and a new kind of somberness, a new watchfulness, replaced the one that we New Yorkers had been living with in the weeks following the attack. I don't know whether my rereading of the poem in the light of the terrible event can hold water far beyond that event, or whether, when I read it the way I did, it was my intelligence at work rather than the universal feelings of depression and powerlessness working on me; somehow, as I passed further into what people insist is a new world, "Song of Myself" just seemed more inscrutable than I had ever given it credit for being, and even richer and more profound. "I too am untranslatable," Whitman says at the end, and he is probably right. But seeing the poem in the way I saw it helped me. It gave me a way to hold the event in my mind, to come closer to it and not be afraid. I'm grateful to the poem, and to the coincidences that required me to reread it.

———

I had some more commerce with Whitman in the aftermath of the attack. That October, I read from him at one of the many memorial events in New York. I had only five minutes—many people were reading—so I chose some passages from "Crossing Brooklyn Ferry." The passage I ended with was this one:

> *Ah, what can ever be more stately and admirable to me than mast-hemm'd Manhattan?*
> *River and sunset and scallop-edg'd waves of flood-tide?*
> *The sea-gulls oscillating their bodies, the hay-boat in the twilight, and the belated lighter?*
> *What gods can exceed these that clasp me by the hand, and with voices I love call me promptly and loudly by my nighest name as I approach?*
> *What is more subtle than this which ties me to the woman or man that looks in my face?*
> *Which fuses me into you now, and pours my meaning into you?*
>
> *We understand then do we not?*
> *What I promis'd without mentioning it, have you not accepted?*
> *What the study could not teach—what the preaching could not accomplish is accomplish'd, is it not?*

Kid Roberts and Me

The Leather Pushers, by H. C. Witwer

. C. Witwer's 1920 novel *The Leather Pushers* went for a song at a recent auction of boxing books and ephemera at New York's Swann Galleries. One of six books in Lot 51, which included Budd Schulberg's *The Harder They Fall* and Harold Ribalow's *World's Greatest Boxing Stories*, it was not among the sale's more celebrated titles. My paddle was up at eighty dollars, again at ninety, and then I made my mistake. I began to think. Five of the books didn't matter to me, and ninety-five dollars is pretty steep for a book that isn't a collector's item. On the other hand, I had been looking for *The Leather Pushers* for fifteen years, which comes to about seven dollars a year, counting the buyer's premium. While I was considering all this, the lot was sold to a man one row in front of me for a hundred dollars.

Had I been wearing ten-ounce gloves, I would have beaten myself up. I was a piker, a cheapskate, a dope. But perhaps all was not lost. During the break I approached the newest owner of *The Leather Pushers* and wondered whether he might consider parting with it for a fair price. Naturally, he cocked his head at this. Did I know something he did not? Having satisfied himself that I was neither a collector nor a dealer, merely an eccentric, this splendid fellow, a partner in the brokerage house of McFadden, Farrell & Smith, announced that he would make a present of it. I, of course, wouldn't hear of such a thing. He, of course, would hear of nothing else. A week later Witwer's novel arrived in the mail.

An exultant moment, yet not without a vague anxiety. Suddenly I wasn't sure that I wanted to revisit a book I had left behind such a long time ago. Instead of devouring it, I was content simply to handle it, a well-preserved 1921 cloth edition of 341 pages with a cover illustration of two fighters flailing against a splattered red-and-white background. True, I could not resist glancing occasionally at the first paragraph, which to my relief was competently written; but then I'd put the book aside, as if not to push my luck. Finally, after a few nights of dithering, I took it to bed. I surged past the first paragraph, the first page, the second, and gradually it came to me: the reason that I had hunted it down long after forgetting just about everything in it.

To be honest, I had even forgotten the book's title and author. This was a novel I had last read in 1961, when I was fourteen, and aside from the hero's name—his ring name: Kid Roberts—all I could remember was that he had gone to

Harvard; that his tycoon father naturally deplored his brutal vocation; that the beautiful and classy girl who loved him also deplored his brutal vocation; and that Harvard notwithstanding, the Kid went on to become the heavyweight champion of the world. I was fourteen, what did I know?

Maybe because it had been borrowed from a classmate or maybe because the sixties had efficiently sutured off my adolescence, I forgot all about the novel. So complete was its obliteration that I actually picked up a paperback copy of *The Leather Pushers* at the auction preview without any bells going off. Only the name "Kid Roberts" on the back cover alerted me to the fact that *this* was the book. A moment later, the cloth edition turned up.

Recovering memories is a mysterious process. Fifteen years earlier, while I was explaining to a bemused young woman my interest in boxing and boxing literature, the name Kid Roberts, without warning, without the slightest tectonic shift in memory, suddenly burst from oblivion. One moment the book wasn't there, the next instant it was, and though the characters and plot were all muddled, I remembered distinctly how it felt to have read it. I was nuts about the book. It was what stories and reading stories were all about. And by God, I was going to find it.

I saw myself as a svelte Caspar Gutman traveling the world over in search of the black bird. But without benefit of title or author, mine was a rather messy quest. I asked around—but the people who knew literature didn't know beans about boxing books, and the people who knew boxing didn't read all that much. I checked out every secondhand bookstore in every city I visited, looking for—well, anything that might lead me further. I found plenty of rare books that way, including a copy of Conan Doyle's *The Croxley Master and Other Tales of the Ring and Camp*, but no novels about a fighter named Kid Roberts. One winter afternoon in the multi-lampshaded reading room of the New York Public Library, I ran my eye down tiny-lettered columns in old volumes of *Books in Print*. What was I looking for?

In time a search takes on a life of its own. Unless the longed-for object is of inherent value—a jewel-encrusted falcon—it becomes secondary to the search itself. *The Leather Pushers* was just a book, but it was a book I read when there had been no end to novels every bit as wonderful as those by H. C. Witwer, when practically every novel that fell into my hands seemed absolutely right. At fourteen, I read quickly, furiously, compulsively. I went through five, six novels a week or suffered from withdrawal. Reading at this pace is not unique among the bookish young, but as with any obsession, there is something faintly suspect about it, as if the allure of books indicts the world's ability to deliver an equivalent amount of pleasure or meaning.

Love of reading, or a reading dependency, is a phenomenon often acknowledged by those incapable of stopping. In *Reading: An Essay*, one of five small books in J. B. Priestley's Pleasures of Life series, Hugh Walpole divides readers into two general categories: the ecstatic and the critical, allowing of course for the inevitable overlap. Whether one becomes one kind of reader or the other, according to Walpole, depends on "some dominating influence" that appears in the life of every future reader, usually at the age of fourteen or fifteen, "that solves, partly, the question as to whether he will be in later life an aesthetic or unaesthetic reader."

For Walpole, it was Walter Scott's Waverley novels that sent him tumbling down the ecstatic path. Scott did it for me too, but he had help from Rafael Sabatini, Alexandre Dumas *père*, Victor Hugo, Robert Louis Stevenson, James Fenimore Cooper, Jules Verne, Jack London, the two Edgars—Allan Poe and Rice Burroughs—and, yes, H. C. Witwer. Fourteen seems to be a magic age for the confirmed reader. In "The Lost Childhood," his short essay on becoming a writer, Graham Greene asked:

> What do we ever get nowadays from reading to equal the excitement and the revelation in those first fourteen years? Of course I should be interested to hear that a new novel by Mr. E. M. Forster was going to appear this Spring, but I could never compare that mild expectation of civilized pleasure with the missed heartbeat, the appalled glee I felt when I found on a library shelf a novel by Rider Haggard, Percy Westerman, Captain Brereton or Stanley Weyman.

When Greene was fourteen, his library shelf delivered up Marjorie Bowen's novel *The Viper of Milan* and "for better or worse the future was struck. From that moment [he] began to write." Much as I'd like to say that *The Leather Pushers* made me into a writer, or even a golden-glove novice, I'm afraid it wouldn't be true. Still, I can recall "the missed heartbeat, the appalled glee" I felt when the sequel to *The Three Musketeers* fell into my clutches. To be young was bookish heaven. At fourteen I read every word of every page; I didn't know you *could* skip words. Why should I when all authors were infallible; all narrators, reliable; every detail, essential? Digressions simply did not exist. Even the famously long dissertation on the battle of Waterloo in *Les Misérables* was enthralling, as timely and material as any other scene.

And reading was fun—not serious fun, mind you, but sequestered, magical, self-absorbed fun. Nothing mattered but the story: who won, who survived, who ended up happy, who came up short. Moreover, all novels—adventure, historical, and fantasy—were on a par; all were equally good. If someone had told me then that the books featuring Tarzan, Scaramouche, the Count of Monte Cristo, Ivanhoe, Jean Valjean, Long John Silver, and Kid Roberts had been written by a single person using seven pseudonyms, I would have concurred at once.

Not that I entirely agree with Walpole. The nature of reading is less definitive than Walpole's claims for it. Sure, there are intoxicated readers, but the high is modulated by the years. Once the young reader gets past the stage where the brain sucks in books as if they were bubbles of oxygen, he or she begins to sense that Melville is doing something different from Steinbeck, and that Dickens and Balzac resemble each other in certain respects, but not in all. As children, we crossed wide-eyed and trusting into the writer's world; as adults, we invite the writer into ours and hold him accountable for how he behaves there.

Walpole erred on the side of optimism, trusting too much in the ecstatic reader's resilience. Surely brevity is part of the ecstatic condition, and by omitting to put temporal brackets around ecstasy, Walpole conveniently forgot that reading evolves (devolves?) into the more or less critical. Schooling and swooning don't mesh, and once we begin to differentiate the rhetorical devices that stylistically and thematically inform different narratives, the innocence, the thrill, and the trusting acceptance disappear. Replaced, to be sure, by the edifying feeling that one is learning something valuable. And of course there is pleasure to be had from analysis, but it is a more complicated pleasure than giving oneself over completely to stories. However you slice it, reading critically is a more solemn affair than reading ecstatically.

"The books one reads in childhood, and perhaps most of all bad and good bad books," George Orwell mused, "create in one's mind a sort of false map of the world, a series of fabulous countries into which one can retreat at odd moments." At fourteen I think I knew that boxing was not a happy or noble profession, but books about it did, in fact, become fabulous countries. From *The Leather Pushers* I went on to find Nat Fleischer's *Pictorial History of Boxing*, which steered me to W. C. Heinz's *Fireside Book of Boxing*, which drew me to biographies of John L. Sullivan and Joe Louis; and eventually I encountered the marvelous A. J. Liebling and, through Liebling, Pierce Egan, the first chronicler of the London Prize Ring.

Those repelled by boxing, or simply indifferent, may be surprised to learn of the vast literature devoted to it. R. A. Hartley's *History and Bibliography of Boxing Books* mentions twenty-one hundred pugilistic titles published in the English language. One finds in it such names as Thackeray, Dickens,

Byron, Hazlitt, Shaw, Conan Doyle, and Arnold Bennett. American authors are represented by Jack London, Nelson Algren, James T. Farrell, Heywood Broun, Hemingway, Mailer, and Joyce Carol Oates. Witwer merits nine entries, which are immediately followed by four from P. G. Wodehouse. So many scribes of the scuffle, one ponders, so many literary eminencies drawn to the sport.

So who was H. C. Witwer? I didn't know. I didn't even know what his initials stood for, since the 1921 Grosset & Dunlap edition I now owned neglected to say. But I knew where to look. Page 290 of volume 21 of *The National Cyclopaedia of American Biography* shows one column of seventy-five lines for Harry Charles Witwer—not a bad testimonial for a writer no one remembers. Of German extraction, Witwer was born in 1890 in Athens, Pennsylvania, and died thirty-nine years later in Los Angeles. A short life, but one that netted him a considerable reputation as journalist, humorist, fiction writer, and screenwriter. As a young man in Philadelphia, Witwer held down a bunch of odd jobs—errand boy, hotel clerk, salesman, fight manager—before landing a position with the *St. Cloud* (Florida) *Tribune*. From there he moved on to the *New York American*, the *Brooklyn Eagle*, and the *New York Sun*, for which he covered the First World War.

"Meantime his attempts to write conventional magazine fiction in correct English were unsuccessful," moralizes *The National Cyclopaedia*. "Ordinary language failed him as an effective vehicle for his vein of humor." Indeed, had it not been for Mrs. Witwer, clearly an estimable woman and critic, *The Leather Pushers* might never have become my pugilistic Rosebud. It was she who "finally set him on the right path by suggesting that he write as he spoke," the result being an "unexampled outflow of slang stories . . . and with the first one printed he won the interest of the large American reading public which prefers its fiction in the vernacular." During a fifteen-year period, Witwer published four hundred stories, twenty-five screenplays, fourteen novels, and four plays. *Whew*, to use the vernacular.

When Mrs. Witwer advised her husband to write as he spoke, she was clearly giving the raspberry to Comte de Buffon's dictum that "those who write as they speak, even though they speak well, write badly." Knowing instinctively that such a rule applies less scrupulously if one speaks like a mook to begin with, Mrs. Witwer urged her husband on. A good thing too. Witwer's prose is brisk, workmanlike, and certainly superior to that found in the story weeklies, dime novels, and hundreds of pulp magazines that catered to the tastes of a vernacular-preferring public:

Me and Cockeyed Egan was tourin' "God's Own Country" (Russian for the West), where the natives would rather be Harold Bell Wright than be president, each with a stable of battlers, picking up *beaucoup* sugar by havin' 'em fight each other over the short routes, when Kane Halliday skidded across my path. Besides Beansy Mullen and Bearcat Reed, a coupla heavies, I had a good welter in Battlin' Lewis, and Egan had K. O. Krouse, another tough boy, which made up a set. Them

last two babies mixed with each other more times a month
than a chorus girl uses a telephone.

Although Witwer wrote about the sharpies, hustlers,
louts, and swaggerers of the sporting world, he wrote about
them with élan. Loftiness is a question more of style than of
substance. And perhaps with the good Mrs. Witwer proofing
the pages as they rolled off the Underwood, H.C. mined a
vein of hard-boiled prose that appealed to the audience that
pshawed the pulps. He wrote with a wink and a nudge, his
style an implicit compact between author and reader in which
each knows better than the malapropisms and solecisms that
bedeck the printed page. In short, we and Witwer are in ca-
hoots. Twain had already led the way with Tom and Huck,
and if Harry Witwer is no Mark Twain, neither is he any less
proficient than Damon Runyon at conjuring up an urban
America that was beginning to strut its stuff in books and
movies. The obvious resemblance, of course, is to his exact
contemporary Ring Lardner, who, although a more serious
and more subtle comic writer, might have no cause to resent
comparison.

Having now reread *The Leather Pushers*, I am amazed at
how much must have gone right by me. Who in blazes is
Harold Bell Wright, and why would some people rather be
him than be president? (Wright was a bestselling novelist
ninety years ago, author of *The Winning of Barbara Worth*
and *The Shepherd of the Hills*, which romanticized the lives

of country folk.) Other allusions to historical figures and events—"He won more gold and silver cups than the Crown Prince lifted from Belgium"—also could have made no sense to a fourteen-year-old. But what did it matter? The prose had verve, it had attitude. The Kid is introduced:

> This guy had been committed to college with the idea that when he'd come out he'd be at the very least a civil engineer, though most of the engineers I know learned their trade in a round-house and yard and was civil enough as far as that part of it goes. Halliday's people was supposed to have a dollar for every egg in a shad roe, and the boy treated the civil engineer thing as a practical joke and college as somethin' he had been gave for Christmas to play with.

I can't say I'm all agog, but I do see how an adolescent male would find something terrifically adult about this kind of writing. Of course, at fourteen I also thought the narrator just a means to an end, a way of getting to the real story of Kid Roberts, whose actual name is the phony-sounding Kane Halliday. The truth is that the narrator is more likable and more interesting than his highborn hitter. Kane Halliday is that stock character in popular novels of the period, "the Gentleman"—noble as the day is long, a defender of women, a dutiful son, a boon companion, and as brave a man as ever fastened on a pair of spats. In short, the Kid's a snore.

At fourteen, however, I must have admired him enormously. In fact, it says something that thirty-five years later I could be disappointed at hearing him admit: "When I first went into this game, I made up my mind that under no circumstances would I ever step into a ring with a colored man.

Never mind my reasons—they're ethical and my own." But the Kid does fight a black man because "a real champion should bar *no* one, whether it be a contest of brains or brawn."

A little of this kind of rhetoric goes a long way, though never toward making a character likable. Halliday sounds like a caffeinated Edward Everett Horton, but without the grace to look foolish while declaiming on this or that outrage. Witwer may have been giving his audience what it expected from someone who had all the advantages except knowing what life was all about, but the Kid's formal speech grates rather than amuses. Speaking of speaking, an irony almost too good to be true is that a few years after the novel's publication, an actual boxer appeared on the scene— Gene Tunney by name—who, tough enough to outpoint Jack Dempsey twice, resorted, especially when the press was around, to loony locutions that he regarded as college-speak.

Will I now go on to read or reread Witwer's thirteen other novels, including *Fighting Back*, the sequel to *The Leather Pushers*? Probably not, though *From Baseball to Boches* and *The Classics in Slang* make tempting titles. My search, after all, is over. I have my book and I've read it too. And I learned something. I learned that Kid Roberts didn't actually like to fight; he fought because his father made some unsound investments and lost the family fortune. Nor, as it turns out, did Dad disapprove of his son's profession; in fact, he got a kick out of it. As for the beautiful, classy young woman, a senator's daughter, even she rooted for the big educated palooka when he stepped between the ropes. Oh, it was Yale the Kid went to, not . . . I mean, a heavyweight champion from Harvard? Come on.

So memory has been corrected. But there is more than a tinge of melancholy in such emendation. Neither the book nor its youthful reader can ever exist for each other in quite the same way. *The Leather Pushers* is dated, long-winded, not without its dull patches. The same might be said of its middle-aged reader. But something else can be said as well. For just a few minutes while paging through the novel, I sensed through the haze of years and the intellectual veil lowered by critics and well-intentioned professors what it was like to read as if there were no tomorrow. The pure joy of reading may never be regained, but if we're lucky, we can chance across one of those "good bad books" we read thirty or forty years ago and recall what it's like to be a child who reads. Such books are like old snapshots taken at the age when the baby fat is just swimming off the bone, when the personality is just beginning to acknowledge what it will find forever interesting, when the eyes begin to reveal for the first time the person who will be using them for the rest of his life.

My Life with a Field Guide

A Field Guide to Wildflowers of Northeastern and North-Central North America,
by Roger Tory Peterson and Margaret McKenny

was seventeen when it started. My family was on vacation in Maine, and one day we went on a nature walk led by a young man a few years older than I. Probably I wanted to get his attention—I'm sure I did—so I pointed to a flower and asked, "What's that?"

"Hmmm? Oh, just an aster," he said.

Was there a hint of a sniff as he turned away? There was! It was just an aster and I was just a total ignoramus! The tidal weight of my blithering ignorance was a thing I remember clearly, even now.

And I remember the aster. Its rays were a brilliant purple, its core a dense coin of yellow velvet. It focused light as a crystal will. It faced the sun, rigid with delight; it was the sun's echo.

Later that day, a book with a green cover lay on the arm of an Adirondack chair under an apple tree. It was the same volume that our guide had carried as he marched us through the woods. Everyone who had been on the walk had gone into the nature center for milk and cookies, and the book had been left there, by itself. It was a thing of power, as totemic in its way as an orb and scepter. In the thin summer shadow of the tree, quivering, like a veil—green on green on green—the book was revealed, and I reached for it. A FIELD GUIDE TO WILDFLOWERS—PETERSON & McKENNY, its cover said. Its backside was ruled like a measuring tape, its inside was full of drawings of flowers. By the end of that week I had my own copy. I have it still.

Over the next several years this field guide would become my closest companion, a slice of worldview, as indispensable, finally, as eyes or hands. I didn't arrive at this intimacy right away, however. This wasn't going to be an easy affair for either of us. And—unlike other love affairs—our liaison began in a way that gave no pleasure at all.

I'll give you an example of how it went. After I'd owned the Peterson's for about a week, I went on a hike with some friends up a little mountain in Maine, taking the book along. Halfway up the mountain, there by the trailside was a yellow flower, a nice opportunity to take my new guide for a test drive. "Go on ahead!" I said to my hiking companions. "I'll be a minute . . ." Famous last words.

I had already figured out (intuitive, isn't it?) the business of the colored tabs. I turned in an authoritative way to the Yellow part and began to flip through. By the time the last of my friends had disappeared up the trail, I'd arrived at a page where things looked right. Five petals? Yes. Pinnate leaves? Whatever. Buttercup? There are, amazingly, *eleven* buttercups. Who would have thought? However hard I tried to make it so, my item was not one of them. Next page. Aha! This looked more like it. Bushy cinquefoil? Nope, leaves not *quiiite* right, are they? As the gnats descended, I noticed that there were six more pages ahead, each packed with five-petaled yellow flowers—St. Johnsworts, loosestrifes, puccoons. *Puccoons! What the . . . heck! I'll do this some other time!* I started up the trail, swatting away, at which point I realized that I couldn't hear my friends anymore, and began to run. The trail forked, and there were a few bad moments before I caught up to the group, sitting by a streamside sipping from water bottles. By that time I was hot and in a foul mood and still gripping the culprit—the consarned book.

I was tempted to can the whole thing right there. I was tempted to do this many times, in fact. Even if I didn't heave the book into the underbrush, I could have taken it home and put it on a shelf, which would have amounted to the same thing.

Why I persisted in carrying it around and consulting its crowded pages at every opportunity, I have no idea. The book was stubborn; well, I was stubborn too; that was part of it. And I had no choice, really, not if I wanted to *get in*. A landscape may be handsome in the aggregate, but this book led to the particulars, and that's what I wanted. A less complete guide would have been easier to start with, but more frustrating in the end. A more complete book—one of the official Floras—would have been impossible for me to use. So I continued to wrestle with the Peterson's, and thus by slow degrees the crowd of plant stuff in the world became composed of individuals. As it did, the book changed: its cover was stained by water and snack food, the spine grew invitingly lax, some of the margins sprouted cryptic annotations.

By the time the next summer came, I had bought the field guide some accompaniments: bug dope and a hand lens and a small notebook. I had fully discovered the joy of the hunt, and every new species had its trophy of data—name and place and date—to be jotted down. If I'd found a flower before, I was happy to see it again, just as one is uplifted by the singing of a familiar hymn. I often addressed it with enthusiasm: *Hi there, Solidago hispida!* I did this silently, of course, but as I've gotten older and less inhibited, I've sometimes forgotten myself and let fly. And why not? I discovered early on that a plant's Latin name is a name of power by which it can be uniquely identified among different spoken tongues, across continents, and through time. The genus name lashes it firmly to its closest kin, while its species name describes a personal attribute—*rubrum* meaning red, *officinale* meaning medicinal, *odoratus* meaning smelly, and so on. It all makes such delightful sense! The Latin rolls off the tongue in a satisfying way, a fossil language that is still, here in the Realm of Living Things, alive and liquid and irreducible.

For a while I was curious about that single letter that plants have after their binomial—rather like British peers, I thought—and was amused to find out that this was the initial of the sainted immortal who had "discovered" the species and named it for posterity. Though the Peterson's lacks this sophistication, other botany texts include it, and at that time I was meticulous in noting it down. I remember climbing Mount Washington the summer after I bought the Peterson's (I see this from my notebook) and finding the pincushion plant, *Diapensia lapponica L.* By then I knew that *L* stood for Carolus Linnaeus, the Swedish botanist who invented this luscious nomenclature more than two centuries ago. He named this very plant, himself, from a specimen that must have come "from Lapland" (*lapponica*)—and here it was in New Hampshire! I stood there on the peak, hair streaming in the wind (metaphorically speaking; knowing the weather for which the White Mountains are famous, I was probably hunched in the fog). I had entered the land of the musk ox and the reindeer, the circumpolar North, and hovered in the presence of the Great Botanist Himself. His *Diapensia* bloomed at my feet, each mound so neat and white that my retinas effervesced with joy.

Somewhere in its second year, the book's dust jacket, with all its pretty colors, began to disintegrate. I tore it up and used the bits to mark sites of future searches and past victories. When I ran out of dust jacket, I used whatever came handy—sticks, matchbook covers, strips torn from a package of peanut M&M's. This became part of the field guide's natural habiliments, a frill of bookmarks, like the topknot of a distressed parrot.

I became more successful at identifying plants in the field, though my hiking companions still tended to be mystified by my enthusiasms. Three years later I climbed the same little mountain—in the Camden Hills in Maine—where I had carried the Peterson's on its first outing. The yellow flower was still there by the trailside.

"*Geum virginianum!*" I pantingly announced (the delightful little rough avens—best identified from the White section, even though this one *was* Yellow).

"Jim who?" said someone.

"Virgin *what?*" snorted another.

In wintertime, while the book rested on a shelf, the green of its spine was a consolation, promising that the weather would one day be warm and that I would be out in it. Finally I decided that I was not out in it enough, so in the early 1970s I moved to a farm in rural Vermont. The back-to-the-land movement was at its height, and for some of us who were of college and draft age, rural hardships seemed better than alternatives elsewhere. What I remember was our pride in growing vegetables and cutting wood, our desire for everything natural. So during that first summer in the Green Mountains, I went to the local college and signed up for a course in field ecology.

The first day of class I met Julie, another refugee from points south who—miracle of miracles!—shared my interest in rambling around outdoors. Three afternoons a week, after class, we took field trips of our own. We followed river valleys and plunged into bogs and climbed mountains without worrying too much about inclement weather or property boundaries. We always took the Peterson's along. After a while it wasn't enough for us just to name things; we wanted to know what they were good for. So the guide got cross-referenced to *Culpeper's Complete Herbal* and to *Sturtevant's Edible Plants of the World* and—when questions of identity were dicey—to the college's herbarium. Our houses filled with rustling bunches of drying herbs—self-heal, yarrow, mullein, goldenseal, boneset, bergamot. Our neighbors thought these were, you know, drugs or something, which I suppose they were. We compounded herb teas with which we dosed ourselves and our long-suffering friends; every bunch of field flowers on a kitchen table became an opportunity for declamations in Latin; swims in the local pond were voyages of discovery to insect-eating sundews, rare stands of wild azaleas, peculiar bladderworts floating on balls of captured air. At night I would pore over the pages of my Peterson's, catching up on my notes, studying the shapes and habitats of unfamiliar plants so that I might recognize them when I saw them in the flesh. Surprisingly, this often worked. I would notice the latest grail as soon as it hove into view and would fling myself on it with a cry of recognition. That summer, my field guide got the greatest sustained workout of its long life. Its pages grew spotted with plant juice from having specimens thrust into them, annotations threatened to swamp the text, and the cover began, ever so gently, to decorticate from the binding.

The book got used, of course, after that, but not with such intensity. It isn't that we actually found everything in there— oh my God no! It would take a dozen summers like that one, as unfettered as we were, to *find* all the flowers in that book. And the book is not complete, we discovered that. There's more out there than you can imagine—more than anyone could encompass—some of it rare, much of it secretive, all of it meaningful.

We identified individual plants in our rambles, but from the particulars we began to know wholes. Bogs held one community, montane forests held another, and the plants they held in common were clues to intricate dramas of climate change and continental drift. So from plant communities it followed that the grand schemes of things, when they came our way, arrived rooted in real place and personal experience: quaternary geology, biogeography, evolutionary biology all lay on the road that we had begun to travel.

In the next few years, both of us would earn undergraduate degrees in botany. Julie went on to get her Ph.D. and was hired by the Soil Conservation Service; I grew by stages into a nature writer and illustrator. Both of us think of that wild summer as having been the real beginning of our careers.

By the time summer came to an end, the wildflower guide had been joined by one of the official Floras, plus other volumes from the Peterson series: *Trees and Shrubs*, *Ferns*, *Animal Tracks*, *Birds*—those were early ones. Nowadays, as I pass my half-century mark, my bookshelves are full of biological reference works. There are handbooks and encyclopedias and vintage tomes, boxes of periodicals and papers and diskettes, field guides to an array of subjects and places. In all this diversity, plant and flower guides still have the upper hand. And among these, my original *Field Guide* to *Wildflowers of Northeastern and North-Central North America*—its full title—reigns as the great-grandmarm. It's in smithereens now and buckled by damp, held together with a trio of rubber bands. In spite of its copious annotations and cross-references, I tend to use a newer model, though I do take the old one along from time to time, just to let it smell the *Diapensia*, so to speak, much as I might take an arthritic family dog for a ramble, out of kindness, and because of happy memories of adventurous times when both of us were less marked up.

Rereading this book has been interesting, partly because I never really read it to begin with. Not beginning to end, like other books. I studied it, argued with it, carried it around— but I didn't read it. Well, I've read it now! In the process, I've discovered a couple of things that I never knew were there.

First of all, in the introduction, I discovered a Roger Tory Peterson that I didn't know existed. I met him a time or two; he was an acquaintance of my father's, and his son was a friend of mine. I thought of him as a grand old man, an artist, somewhat supercilious, perhaps, but why shouldn't he have been? I'd never thought of him as actually *doing* writing or illustrating, not the way I did. But here he is, in the introduction, getting talked into making the drawings because the original illustrator was detained in a publishing wrangle. That's exactly what happened to me! That's how I started my own career as an illustrator. By mistake. And look, here he is driving thousands of miles in his station wagon and spending nights in motels drawing his subjects into the wee hours. As for the rare plants—look here: "I often drew them while lying flat on the ground." He was suddenly a colleague, getting dirty, finding—in the light of life—that his book needed to be changed. In the process of drawing, he got an education. As a result, there are more plants in the book than were originally intended, and fewer words. He had no botanical pretensions. He did have an artist's trained eye and he gypsied over the whole territory. So there you are. He drew fifteen hundred plants for this book. I am forever amazed.

They are wonderful drawings, and the very first page of the pictorial guide is, for some reason, chockablock with flowers I know well. I could write an entire essay on the contents of this first page alone, six "WHITE Miscellaneous Flowering Shrubs," all with interesting lifestyles and personal associations. For example, here's Labrador-tea. Its text is particularly crisp:

LABRADOR-TEA   Ledum groenlandicum
HEATH FAMILY   (Ericaceae)
Note the white or rusty *wool on underside* of untoothed leaves.
Leaves leathery, with *rolled edges*; fragrant. A low shrub (to 3
ft.). Cold bogs.
Canada, n. U.S.   MAY–JUNE

Note that it grows in Labrador and that the type specimen likely came from Greenland (*groenland*) and that it's related to the heather on the Scottish moors that were once inhabited by my personal antecedents. Its habitat is also a give-away: this is a tundra denizen that has hung on here under our postglacial spruces. My annotation says: "Bear Swamp 6/12/73." Bear Swamp in Vermont is a kind of botanist's wet dream, filled with rare plants and anomalous associa-tions, and since I lived on its borders for more than twelve years, its name alone conjures up dozens of the most intense memories. I also remember that Labrador-tea was one of the items that Julie and I collected and brewed up. I can still taste it. Though the power of my memory is not what it used to be when it comes to things like dentist appointments and bank balances, my capacity for botanical minutiae seems undiminished. I last saw Labrador-tea just three weeks ago, on Deer Isle in Maine. I remember the path, the autumn light on the dark leaves, and the feel of the tips I reached out to touch as I passed, releasing a cloud of scent. I was tempted to pick some to brew and drink, and resisted.

If this is what the first page conjured up, I think you can see that rereading this book has been like watching my life pass before my eyes. The text is dull for the same reasons that it's so useful in the heat of identification, so I haven't enjoyed the reading part, exactly. But I took pleasure in the drawings. I found myself poring over the images of those plants that I've wanted to find and never have—pasqueflower, whorled pogonia, atamasco-lily—and the creepy ones like dodder and water-dragon. I found fragments of chopstick wrappers and Band-Aid papers doing their duty as bookmarks. I found the aster too. There are forty-four species in the book, but the one that got me started so long ago was a New England aster, *Aster novae-angliae*. It's wonderful enough when it's purple, but the pink form knocks my socks off every time.

The other thing I discovered was a plant that, I swear to you, I have never seen in there before. (This has often happened; I suspect it always will. Little Peterson djinns must come and put new stuff in the field guide overnight.) What I noticed this time was bur cucumber, *Sicyos angulatus*. Though there are only twelve wild cucurbits in the field guide's area, I could tell it was a member of the cucumber family right away. I'm so comfy with most plant families that I can usually assign a plant to its own on sight, a kind of gestalt botanizing that people can find impressive and that can lead me to think I know a thing or two. But this was something new. I studied the drawing: prickly, star-shaped clusters of fruit, very funny-looking. Fat, cucumbery leaves.

Then, just yesterday, I was stopped at a traffic light down by the grade school. A vine was tangled in the fence there. I stared at it with my mouth open while the light turned green and everybody honked at me. There it was, bur cucumber, large as life.

A Companion of the Prophet

Arthur Rimbaud, by Enid Starkie

n New Year's Eve, 1973, I sat on my bed in my room in my parents' house in New Jersey, bawling like an infant. I hadn't cried so hard in years, probably not since turning twelve, when I had made a pact with myself never to cry again. Now I was nineteen and halfway through sophomore year of college. I was sad because I didn't have a girlfriend and hadn't been invited to a party, and because I imagined I was nothing. None of these feelings was new or unexpected, of course. I carried them around routinely; misery and isolation were crucial parts of my self-definition. What drew all the hurt to the surface that night and caused me to dissolve into hot tears was a book I'd read before: Enid Starkie's biography of Arthur Rimbaud. I must have known what I was doing when I pulled it off the shelf, must have deliberately intended to use it as an instrument of mortification. I had to check a date: 1873. By the end of 1873 Rimbaud had finished *A Season in Hell*, which meant he had written all his major works, or very nearly. He would polish off the partly completed *Illuminations* the following year, but by 1875 he had ceased to make or care about literature. The year mattered to me because Rimbaud was born in 1854, at one end of the Ardennes mountains, and I was born in 1954 at the other.

At some point before adolescence, I had decided to become a child prodigy—an ambition probably inspired by garbled reports of the sorts of things that well-meaning teachers tell anxious parents of frustratingly underachieving pupils. I surely possessed gifts, but I daydreamed, wasted time, failed to work. Still, by nine or ten I commanded a vast fund of the kind of knowledge that impresses the pikers— catalogs of trivia. I wasn't one of those scary kids who know everything on earth about snakes or ancient Egypt or the F-111 jet fighter. I was a generalist, with interests in art and history and an age-appropriate obsession with all manifestations of the uncanny; I thought I might someday be a cartoonist or a historian or a researcher of the paranormal. Then, not long before my tenth birthday, a teacher told me I had talent as a writer, and for some reason that changed everything. I suddenly knew what I would be, and even though visual art continued to tug at me, I never really deviated from my course. I knew that I would soon be an impossibly young writer of astounding gifts and wisdom far beyond his years.

I quickly acquired some secondhand books, all of them titled something like *How to Write for Publication*, and had my parents get me a subscription to *Writer's Digest*. These sources gave counsel on how to compose a cover letter, how to begin a factual account with a dramatic anecdote, how to prepare a special calendar to assist in writing seasonally themed sketches six months in advance. I followed their suggestions, submitting light verse to *Gourmet* and historical filler items to *Boating*, and happily collected rejection slips as if they were stamps. Imagining my work being read by busy people in skyscraper offices was a thought imbued with the kind of magic that attended the sending away of box tops in exchange for plastic figurines. I read indiscriminately, Sherlock Holmes and hot-rod novels, UFO exposés and accounts of the Civil War, Dickens and Bob Hope, Horatio Hornblower and *Worlds in Collision*. All of it was literature, and all of it was good. I imagined a worldwide communion of writers past and present seated at their desks, assembling words at the gratifying potential rate of ten cents per, C. S. Forester and Immanuel Velikovsky and Arthur Conan Doyle and Franklin W. Dixon all stamping self-addressed envelopes, filing away carbon copies, letting the steel jaw of the mailbox slap shut while murmuring a little prayer.

Then, at age thirteen, in Montreal with my family for Expo 67, I found myself in a French-language bookstore. For some reason I picked up a fat anthology called *Le livre d'or de la poésie française*, probably because it had been published in my native town in Belgium. I hadn't previously been much interested in poetry, but I was immediately drawn by the fact that the book's latter half was a regular riot of jagged lines, very long lines, very short lines, even entire blocks of prose.

Poetry in regular stanzas, appropriately rhymed and me-
tered, had always appeared obedient, pious, well-groomed,
but this stuff clearly refused to be shepherded into church in
ordered rows. Leafing through the book in search of more, I
found an odd chain of prose passages interspersed with thin
columns of verse. It was headed: "DÉLIRES / ii / Alchimie
du verbe."

My turn. The story of one of my infatuations.

*For a long time I considered myself master of every
possible landscape, and looked down on famous painters and
modern poets.*

*I liked idiotic paintings, doorway moldings, decorative
backdrops, carnival banners, signs, cheap prints; outmoded
literature, Church Latin, illiterate pornography, mildewed
novels, fairy tales, children's books, old operas, silly ditties,
naïve rhythms. I dreamed up crusades, unrecorded voyages of
exploration, republics with no histories, aborted wars of
religion, revolutions in behavior, migrations of races and shifts
of continents: I believed in every kind of magic.*

*I invented the colors of vowels!—A black, E white, I red, O
blue, U green—I set the form and motion of each consonant,
and using intuitive rhythms I decided I had invented a poetic
language that would someday apply to all the senses. I reserved
the translation rights.*

*At first it was an experiment. I wrote silences; I wrote nights;
I jotted down the inexpressible. I froze the dizzying whirl. . . .*

*Poetic castoffs played a major part in my alchemy of the
word.*

*I practiced elementary hallucinations: I clearly saw a
mosque in place of a factory, a school of drummers made up of
angels, coaches on the roads in the sky, a parlor at the bottom of
a lake, monsters, mysteries. A title on a marquee would set
phantasms before my eyes.*

*And then I explained my magical sophistries with
hallucinated words!*

*I ended up thinking my spiritual disorder was sacred. I was
idle, prey to fevers. I envied the bliss of animals: caterpillars,
who stood for the innocence of limbo; moles, for the sleep of
virginity!*

(translation mine)

I understood willed hallucination; I intuited synesthesia
without knowing the word; I knew all about imaginary history and every kind of junk literature. The paragraphs were
unlike anything I had ever read, and they were intended for
me specifically. I leafed back a few pages and found the information: "1854–1891—Poète, né à Charleville." Charleville is
in the French Ardennes, on the Meuse, a river I knew well, and
near the Belgian border, in fact quite close to Bouillon, where
I had cousins. The rest of the biography was mostly lost on
me, aside from a few key words: "Charleroi," "Bruxelles,"
"enfant prodige." There were many points of contact between this Arthur Rimbaud and me. Maybe there was something more to the pattern; maybe I was his echo, his
reincarnation! I bought the book.

That bookstore—all I have now is a vague impression of
a large, fluorescent-lit, faintly antiseptic room, like the library of a technical institute—looms in retrospect like Ali
Baba's cave. I left with two books (the other was André Breton's
Anthologie de l'humour noir, bought under a fortuitous mis-
impression), and together they furnished me with my permanent literary foundation; Rimbaud was not the only figure
I encountered as a result. I was thirteen, and it was the

Summer of Love, and the world and I were changing in synchrony. Girls and music and cigarettes and discontent were all happening to me; just out of my reach were sex and drugs and politics, and glamour and fame and the wide world. A year later I won a scholarship to a Jesuit high school in New York City, and the wide world let me in. Every morning I would take a seven o'clock train from the little clapboard suburban station where I was the anomaly in a crowd of suits, and an hour and a half later I stood in the middle of everything. The school quickly came to seem rather beside the point.

I don't know whether it sounds more like a boast or an admission to say that I have always been a good student as long as I was setting the lessons myself. In school I slept or doodled or looked out the window or fine-tuned my fantasy life. Such activities could not sustain Greek or trigonometry, however, and after a while I was expelled. But outside of school I was an eager pupil. I learned from walking around the city, from sitting in cafeterias, from going to the movies, from reading anything that landed under my nose. I learned in bookstores, especially in Wilentz's Eighth Street Bookshop, the beacon of literary hipness in the Manhattan of the 1960s. I had little money to buy books, so I read snatches of them on the spot; and books led me to other books, sometimes just through physical proximity.

I was armed with a nice chunk of Christmas money, at least five and perhaps as much as ten dollars, one day in late 1968 or early 1969 when I walked into the bookstore big-eyed with expectation. At long last I was in a position to buy something, and at first I was dazzled, wanting to take home everything from *Narcissus and Goldmund* to *A Child's Garden of Verses for the Revolution*, the euphoria giving way to calculation and then to disappointment. What, finally, was good enough for me to spend actual money on? And then I saw a thick New Directions paperback—those deadpan black-and-white covers still call to me from across a room—with a picture of a big-haired, pensive, beautiful adolescent: *Arthur Rimbaud* by Enid Starkie. I grandly forked over $3.25 for it. I still didn't know much about Rimbaud. I had read the four works in the anthology I possessed—"Ma bohème," "Le bateau ivre," and "Voyelles," in addition to the excerpt from *A Season in Hell*—again and again with emotions ranging from puzzlement to the sort of excitement that made me actually get up and do an awkward little dance, but their author was represented in neither my town's library nor my school's. It was overwhelming to have nearly five hundred pages about him, complete with pictures.

I read the book slowly, in part because it was dense and in part because I wanted to be seen reading it. I wore the book as much as I read it, "absentmindedly" holding it in one hand on the street even when I was carrying a satchel of books in the other, "casually" parking it atop my notebook next to my coffee cup wherever I sat. I proudly displayed it on the subway, at Nedick's and Chock full o'Nuts and the Automat, in garment-district cafeterias, at the juice stand in the passage from the IRT to the shuttle at Grand Central, in the bar car of the 5:30 express home (drinkless but trying to outsmoke everybody), maybe once or twice at some dump on

St. Mark's Place that advertised Acapulco Gold ice cream. There was no T-shirt available then, but I was identifying my brand in comparable fashion. Rimbaud, dead for eighty years, was enjoying one of his many rebirths. The Starkie biography, first published in 1938, had only just come out in paperback (along with its bookstore companion, the Louise Varèse translation of Rimbaud's works). His name was being thrown around in all sorts of places, such as interviews with pop stars—I felt a little proprietary, as if I owned him and they were encroaching. And there was that face, of course, the detail of Fantin-Latour's *Coin de table* on the cover and the (second) Carjat photograph within, which matched the work and the life and seemed utterly contemporary. He may be a bit of a conventional cherub in the former, but in the latter he is electric, with flames in those pale eyes. He was hipper than anyone alive.

But if in the fullness of my teenage fantasy I felt I must have been appointed a successor to Rimbaud—on the basis of a few biographical details merely shared by several thousand people—at most times he came to stand as a reproach to my cowardice and mediocrity. Yes, I recognized myself in various aspects of his life. Part of this was the result of a childhood immersion in Catholicism, immediately flung down at puberty and followed by a pursuit of what I imagined was its inverse. I liked to think I was dangerous and terrible, even though the shoplifting, pot smoking, truancy, and masturbation that were all I could muster in this regard would have so impressed no one but my poor unsteady mother. I liked to think I was illuminated, but while I could

generate great clouds of smoke, imagining what my works
would look like on the page and how they would be received,
I couldn't actually write what I imagined. I liked to think
that I, too, could manifest genius in a quick series of slaps
and then suddenly leave the room never to return, stranding
traduced friends and weeping sycophants out on the ice,
flicking aside poetry and culture and civilization like a long
ash on a cigarette, but I couldn't very well leave without having first entered.

My writing was pathetic and Rimbaud was unanswer-
able. He was a changeling, an alien. The deeper I burrowed
into Rimbaud, the less I could see him or put flesh on him. I
fancied that I detected aspects in myself corresponding to
some parts of him I thought I understood, but they were surface elements. He was not like a conventional idol, who will
reliably turn out to be contemptible in private; and even
though he was my age, I couldn't make him into a school-
yard rival whom I could find some way of reducing to tears. I
had made a grave error in choosing Rimbaud as my model—
he wasn't even divisible into parts; you couldn't be half a
Rimbaud. The alternative to being Rimbaud was to be nothing. If I had chosen somebody like Jack Kerouac instead, I
wouldn't have had a problem—him I could see all too read-
ily, laugh at his neuroses, nail all his stupidities with no ef-
fort—but that was exactly why I hadn't chosen him. I read
and admired many other writers, but none was Rimbaud,
who remained a perpetual admonition, a painful constant re-
minder of my failure, his nineteenth-century calendar mocking the years of my life. I quit writing poetry when he did, at

twenty-one—although I only just now realized the coincidence—but there the chronological parallels end. He left France, I stayed in New York; he went to Aden, I moved downtown; he went to Harar, I began to write for magazines; he came home to die, I published my first book.

Rimbaud has been dead for 13 years now, or 113 by everyone else's reckoning. I've read everything he ever wrote several times over, some of it many times, and I still feel as though I'm far from getting to the bottom of much of it, *Illuminations* in particular. I've been to his house in Charleville-Mézières and the museum across the street, and thought that maybe I should have done so as a teenager, since while the artifacts are terribly moving, the way the French have of institutionalizing their dead artists is a wonderful homeopathic antidote to hero worship. Charleville is filled with Rimbaud junk merchandise, and in the suburbs you find here and there a sterile landscape traversed by a Rue Arthur-Rimbaud or a housing project with an immense blowup of the Carjat photograph on the wall of its inner court, and politicians quote him in their speeches, and television presenters cite him as if he had been some stuffed owl in the Academy rather than someone who would have caused them to call the police. Had I been a child in France, I would have been made to memorize "Le dormeur du val," and that would have been the end of it. I wouldn't have paid any attention to the poem and wouldn't have wanted to hear any more about him.

I can reread the Starkie biography today, with him doubly interred, and no longer feel as though I will have to set the book down at some point and go put on music and think hard about something else, because the race is over now. Our parallel has been shattered by time and circumstance. I can contemplate in tranquillity just how wildly outmatched I was. Rimbaud, I see now, was never a kid, or at least never a kid poet. At fourteen he wrote a Latin verse in which Phoebus descends from the heavens to write "TU VATES ERIS" (you shall be a poet) on his brow, but that was merely in the service of rhetorical convention. Kid poets are composed of either wet flopping emotion or hollow technical showing off; and if they are ever to amount to anything, they will as they mature slowly lean out and grab hold of the other branch. Rimbaud arrived fully equipped. And Rimbaud never had a Rimbaud. He killed his idols. He swallowed his influences whole; imitated them while improving upon their work; and if they were still alive, made a point of flinging in their faces the fact that he was better at being them than they were.

I've known a couple of people who have reminded me in some way or another of what Rimbaud must have been like, one of them the painter Jean-Michel Basquiat, who, well before he became famous, seemed to live on a parallel plane, so absorbed in his art and its demands that like a heat-seeking missile he would blithely and apparently unconsciously vaporize anything that stood between him and his target. Rimbaud in the flesh, I can see now, was a snot-nosed pest who talked fast with a grating whine, who made fun of everybody in the room and knew that nobody could successfully answer back or hit him without losing face, who came to

your house and ate everything in the fridge before disap-
pearing abruptly and would come around again only when
you had something he wanted. You would probably have to
have been in love with him to tolerate him for long. Quite
beyond lacking his genius, I could never have been anything
like him. As a teenager I was constructed entirely of doubt,
most of it self-doubt, and I am not much different today. I
am larger and slower and older than Rimbaud, even though
I am technically a century younger. Having outlived him, I
feel like one of those companions of the prophet, those
friends of the brilliant young dead who go on to spend the
rest of their lives reselling their anecdotes and testifying in
documentaries. I remember Rimbaud, all those drunken
nights, I will say, gazing wistfully off camera. And I will
silently realize, not without rancor, that now, finally, I can
tame him.

Three Doctors' Daughters

The Sue Barton Books, by Helen Dore Boylston

n the winter of 2001, my father lay near death in something like the family firm. The teaching hospital in Rochester, New York, in which he was a cardiac patient was where he had trained as a medical student, worked as a doctor, and taught in the medical school. His picture is on the wall in the psychiatric wing. Teaching a course in the nursing school, he met his future wife, my mother. Their five children were born within the hospital walls, and two of them graduated from its medical school.

In the familiar corridors of Strong Memorial Hospital, I lectured my two younger sisters with the bossiness of the firstborn: "The patient has very few visual stimuli. It's important to comb our hair and put on lipstick before we go into Daddy's room." "Even if the patient appears to be unconscious, don't assume he can't hear you." For a while my sisters, one of whom is a pediatrician and the other a family therapist, bore this with patience. Finally, they noted sarcastically that they had missed the years when I had become a nurse. Where was all this expertise coming from?

Everything I know about nursing I learned from the seven Sue Barton books, which I read in the 1950s, from the age of ten until I was twelve or thirteen. These juvenile novels, written by Helen Dore Boylston between 1936 and 1952, covered Sue's career from her studies at Massachusetts General Hospital through her jobs as a visiting nurse in the slums of New York City and a rural nurse in the White Mountains of New Hampshire. Each cover had a picture of Sue, wearing a different, distinctive nurse's cap to indicate her current status.

February turned into March. Our father had survived one heart attack, two strokes, and three operations, but he could not talk, sit up unassisted, or feed himself. Nurses appeared at intervals to press buttons on the flotilla of machines attached to him, to put in lines, to draw blood. They fed him puréed substances so neutralized they came pressed into cunning, identifying molds—a pea pod, a corncob, a carrot. Male and female, the nurses wore colored, pajama-like outfits that would have astonished the starched-white-uniformed Miss Barton. As I watched them, more and more of Sue Barton resurfaced.

Other than the agreeably tradition-soaked life of a nursing student and the maxims that bemused my sisters, my main memory of the books was the dialogue between Sue and Bill Barry. A tall, dark intern who comes to Sue's aid on her first, confusing day in the hospital, Bill becomes her husband, but only after many vicissitudes and four books. To a preadolescent, the sparkle of their conversation—and the sense that the speakers were equals in strength—was irresistible.

Forty years after reading Boylston's series, I remembered it as better written, more mature, more fully rounded than most girls' novels. When I mentioned Sue Barton to women of my generation and they asked, "Was she like Cherry Ames?" (the heroine of another nurse series), I responded with more heat than necessary, *"Don't mention that name in the same breath with Sue Barton!"* This was hardly an original bit of literary criticism, since every reading girl in the 1950s knew the crucial distinction between the Sue Barton series and those devoted to Cherry Ames or Trixie Belden or Nancy Drew: Boylston's books were *library* books, whereas when I asked my local librarian why she didn't stock Nancy Drews, she responded, "Because they don't have enough literary merit." She was right. To lump Nancy and Sue together would have been like equating a synthetic, assembly-line wallet with one hand-sewn of fine Florentine leather.

By midsummer, my father was at home learning to walk, talk, read, and write again at eighty-three. Now that the crisis that had inspired so many memories of Sue was over, rereading her seemed imperative. Not sure whether I was about to burst a bubble, lance a boil, or encounter an old friend, I went to the library's main branch to borrow all seven Sue Bartons.

The Rochester Public Library hasn't kept its checkout cards from the 1950s—a shame, because I'd love to know how many times I placed a Sue Barton title on the golden-syrup-colored wooden counter, signed "Kathy Ashenburg" on a stiff piece of orange paper, and waited for the librarian to stamp my due date. How often did I carry the cellophane-protected books, emblazoned with Sue's "vivid" face (a favorite Boylston epithet), out of the branch library on Monroe Avenue? From there it was a short walk down Dartmouth Street to our house, a big clapboard Queen Anne behind a porch with Ionic columns.

In the summers I read on that generous porch, in other seasons in my bedroom. My parents had given me a dark green easy chair that I placed against the window overlooking the backyard—a spot from which, unseen, I could watch the neighborhood kids ringing the kitchen bell and hear my mother calling, "Barbara and Mary want you to play!" I usually wanted to read instead. I think I first encountered Sue Barton in that easy chair, but I'm not certain. The intensity of reading made its own place; I entered the pages and became oblivious to my real surroundings. How many times did I read the books? It seems improbable that the almost-clairvoyant precision with which I recall Boylston's dialogue and descriptions was the result of only one or two readings, but it may well have been. The time-altering passage a child makes into the landscape of certain books may inscribe them permanently in a single journey.

When I reread them, the smallish library books still fitted neatly into my hands, as if I were shrugging into an old jacket that preserved the memory of my elbows and shoulders. I knew those thick pages with their deep bottom margins and dash-filled dialogue, even their smell—an amalgam of paper, thread, libraries, and young girls. The nursing tradition and the life of a great hospital they evoked were as rich as I remembered. The repartee between Sue and Bill Barry, while not up to Noël Coward's standards, still struck a stylish but authentic note:

> Then Barry said, smiling, "You do like me a little—still, don't you?"
>
> "I can bear you," said Sue, lightly. "I even admire you—sometimes—though I'm sure it's presumptuous of me, when there are so many and better nurses to worship at your feet."
>
> He grinned. "I was hoping you'd noticed that!"
>
> "Dear me, how you do hate yourself! And would you kindly tell me what you think you've got except your elegant black hair? Where would you be if you were bald—or even if it were rumpled? All women would flee from you."
>
> "You might rumple it, and find out if you want to run," he said, bending over. His dark head was very close—a well-set head on broad shoulders.
>
> "No, indeed," hastily. "I wouldn't dream of it." She was laughing a little.
>
> —*Sue Barton, Senior Nurse*

In spite of lively dialogue, characterization, and atmosphere, the Sue Barton books aren't Shakespeare. They aren't even Madeleine L'Engle or P. L. Travers. Creations of their time, they come with nuance-free stereotypes. Italians are always excitable, Jews worried, "coloured people" willing and gullible. I still enjoy the prank played on a know-it-all student who is sent to procure a neck tourniquet for a thyroid case ("and hurry!"), but the plots of the individual chapters, typically a "scrape" involving Sue and her pals, are often un-convincing. Although my hunch that these were superior ju-venile novels was vindicated, they are, like the curate's egg, excellent only in parts.

While I marveled that I knew these novels better than the book I read last week, I was equally surprised by the things I did not remember—or had never consciously no-ticed. Indifferent to weather and natural settings as a child, I had failed to appreciate that Boylston is a poet of climate and landscape. "At noon the sky came suddenly down," she writes, describing a snowfall on the New Hampshire coast. "It came endlessly, falling straight, and silent except for a little pelt-ing whisper, an interminable sigh. There was no breath of wind—only that white curtain piling downwards forever on sheeted roofs and cotton trees."

Another aspect that had escaped my attention forty years ago was the current of worry that runs through the series, a to-and-fro rumination about a woman's difficulties in com-bining an independent life with marriage, a profession with a family. When Dr. Barry asks the twenty-year-old Sue, not yet a nurse, if she is "still grimly intent on a career," my eye-brows shot up. How could I have missed that? As a girl, I loved Sue's devotion to her work and her relationship with Bill Barry, and didn't notice that she hardly ever had both at once. Something similar would play out in my own life and in the lives of many women in my generation. But when I first read Sue Barton, I did not even know it was a dilemma.

Helen Dore Boylston did, and the timing of her novels is suggestive. The first was published during the Depression, when nursing was one of the few professions immune to the accusation that women were taking jobs from men. Almost from the start, Dr. Barry (whose charm I still cannot resist) wants Sue. She balks, wishing to live before she settles down. Besides, the most fully expressed romance in the series is Sue's attachment to nursing. The encounter quoted above, in which Bill invites Sue to rumple his hair, continues with Sue feeling something close to panic. After she laughingly refuses, Bill asks, "Why not?"

> An odd sensation, almost like fear, stirred within her. "I—I don't know," she said, and looked up at him with eyes in which there was no trace of laughter.
>
> There was a silence.
>
> Then Sue turned back to the window.
>
> "Look," she said a little unsteadily, "the lights are on in the ward now. In a little while the girls will be getting out the supper trays. It's strange, isn't it, to think how many years that has been going on? The people come and go, but they're just the same, really."
>
> "Yes," he agreed, watching her.
>
> They talked for a few minutes: of the hospital; of the work that was being done in the laboratories on pernicious anaemia; of the differences between medicine and surgery. But when Barry went away at last Sue remained, staring out of the window with a troubled face.

It's a finely observed scene—the girl stirred but reluctant, turning in a flurry from what she may love someday to what she loves steadily, the ongoing life of the hospital.

Ultimately love triumphs—temporarily—over Sue's passion for nursing, but Boylston continues building roadblocks to her domestication. Sue dithers, stalls, breaks the engagement; family crises cause further delays. Finally, at the beginning of *Sue Barton, Superintendent of Nurses*, the fifth book, she marries Bill Barry. At the end of that volume, pregnant with "Bill Junior," Sue hands in her resignation. Boylston declared the series over: a married nurse was iffy, a nurse with a baby out of the question. She turned to a new series about a stagestruck girl named Carol Page.

For some reason, Boylston returned to Sue Barton in 1949 and 1952. In two books written at a time when society wanted women at home after the tumult of war, Boylston's ambivalence is unresolved. Trying to accommodate a stay-at-home heroine with three children in *Sue Barton, Neighborhood Nurse*, Boylston reduces her to helping a troubled teenager and improvising the odd tourniquet. (Sue hasn't lost her old sense of humor, though. After one of her plans goes awry, she tells Bill, "Next time remind me to stay at home and edge the dish towels with tatting.") Three years later, in desperation, Boylston gives Dr. Barry a double dose of pneumonia and tuberculosis that conveniently exiles him to a sanatorium, permitting his wife to return to work in *Sue Barton, Staff Nurse*.

As a child, I never wondered about the writer behind the books, but now I was curious. A little research, including the happy discovery of a Sue Barton home page, filled in some of the picture. Born in 1895, Helen Boylston was, like Sue, a native of Portsmouth, New Hampshire, and a doctor's daughter. After graduating from the Massachusetts General Hospital nursing school in 1915, she nursed in France during the First World War. Boylston's *"Sister": The War Diary of a Nurse* appeared in 1927. The central figure—an edited self-portrait, no doubt, but a self-portrait—can contrive an armchair from boards, box covers, and a fence rail ("Thank God Daddy taught me to use carpenters' tools") and falls in and out of love with dispatch, flirting energetically but far from sure she wants to marry. Of one beau, a young officer almost certainly doomed to die, Boylston writes coolly, "We finally parted with all the necessary drama."

In her twenties and thirties, Boylston seesawed between working as a nurse and magazine writer in America and courting adventure in Europe with her friend Rose Wilder Lane, the daughter of Laura Ingalls Wilder, who was not yet famous as the author of the Little House series. Boylston's nickname was Troubles or Troub, and she did her best to live up to it. "She once made the Albanian Prime Minister carry her trunk off the boat and tried to tip him, not knowing who he was," her publishers wrote. "She was shot at for two hours in a ditch in southern Albania owing to a mistake in identity." After two years in Tirana, Boylston was drawn home by the "irresistible lure" of a photograph of a baked potato in an American magazine, and in 1936 she launched the Sue Barton books. One of the first "career series" for girls, they went into multiple editions and translations and sold hundreds of thousands of copies.

In 1942, *Current Biography* illustrated its full-page article on Helen Dore Boylston with a photograph of the forty-seven-year-old holding up a puppy. Short-haired, slim, wearing a military-style jacket, she looks like Greta Garbo playing Queen Christina. *Current Biography* described her as "handsome and youthful, with strong features." Miss Boylston's leisure activities, according to this account, included wood carving and training dogs. "Her favorite sport is long motor trips. She is unmarried."

Were any of those terms—"unmarried," "handsome," "strong features," "wood carving"—*Current Biography*'s code for gay? A twenty-first-century question, and probably a pointless one. Boylston may well have been a heterosexual who realized that for a woman born in 1895, marriage and a yen for adventure made a bad combination. Her last book, a biography of Clara Barton, the founder of the American Red Cross, was written when she was sixty. She died in 1984, in a nursing home, leaving few personal papers.

The triangular relationship among three doctors' daughters—Sue, Helen Dore Boylston, and me—is an unstable one. Sue is the most constant of the three, although even she evolves from book to book. Boylston is the most enigmatic, because there are significant gaps in my knowledge of her. Did she ever want to marry? Why did she resume the series in 1949? Did she change her mind about what would constitute the fullest life for Sue? Chances are I'll never know the answers. As for me, there is no single reader of Sue Barton. Each time I open one of the books, I put on my current spectacles.

When I was a girl, I imagined I would live as my mother did: marry a doctor or a professor and run a household, read, raise children, and read some more. In 1963, when Betty Friedan's *Feminine Mystique* was published, I argued that rearing children while keeping house was not the dreary round Friedan described. Three years later, engaged and enrolled in a Ph.D. program, I had gone over to the other side. Or, more accurately, I had embraced both sides. I was confident that, armed with a doctorate, I would read to my children every night before cooking maddeningly complex recipes from Julia Child. If I had reread *Neighborhood Nurse* and *Staff Nurse* then, I would have scoffed at Sue's dilemma and Boylston's uncertainty. Why couldn't Sue manage nursing, husband, *and* children?

Predictably, my superwoman period proved impossible to sustain. My husband and I, each raised by a full-time wife and mother, hadn't a clue how to build a home without a dedicated housewife. As we were separating, he remarked that a marriage probably couldn't survive two demanding careers. At that, Bill Barry might well have adjusted his pipe and nodded agreement.

These days, with one side of my brain, I read the last two books in the series as social documents, smiling at their unsubtly conveyed values. With the other side—to my surprise—I read them with considerable emotion. Certain contrived scenes can actually bring a lump to my throat.

Neighborhood Nurse, in particular, is Boylston's most enthusiastic hymn to family values, vintage 1949. Almost every

chapter centers on a minor miracle worked by Sue: a bit of
improvised nursing or social work, the discovery that a frac-
tious child has a serious musical talent, the conversion of an
unmaternal artist into the "real mother" her daughter needs.

Treacly and implausible—and yet at some level it works,
at least for me. Partly it's because even when Boylston tips
into propaganda, she's too fair to render it completely in
black and white, partly because Sue is as wry as an Angel in
the House could be. But mostly, I admit, I respond to the
idyll—the intelligent, happy mother in the big white house,
always available to decipher a tantrum, devise a picnic, haul
an errant twin in from the roof. A rosy-colored picture, but
familiar to someone whose nurse-mother ran a big gray clapboard house for her doctor-husband and five children. I now
see that the Barrys were a wittier version of my own parents,
just as I see that the medical background struck more chords
than I was capable of acknowledging in the 1950s. The hospital is, after all, part of the Ashenburg family romance.

The family romance continues, only now my father—who,
remarkably, has fully recovered—is the nurse. The wife whose
Phi Beta Kappa key he pointed to proudly (his own marks
were never as high as hers) has Alzheimer's. These days my
father cooks and cleans for her, doles out her pills, makes sure
she uses shampoo when she washes her hair—the kind of
age-old, compassionate care Sue Barton gives her patients.

So my mother's situation gives me another reason to appreciate *Neighborhood Nurse*. But even without that motive,
I suspect I warm to it because the life it describes was, if not
a good idea, at least a good dream. For my mother, the choice

to stay home seems to have been relatively uncomplicated; for Sue, more complicated; for me, even more so. For most women of my generation, whichever decision we made was tinged with regret—faint or strong. Regret is probably inevitable when one is balancing two such fundamental things as work and child rearing, and I say that without wanting to re-do my daughters' childhoods with a working mother.

And Helen Dore Boylston's position remains unknown. In the last of the series, she goes to extraordinary plot lengths to get Sue back in the hospital. She sacrifices Bill Barry's health to Sue's temporary return to her career, but he recovers. At the end of the book, before Sue knows that his release from the sanatorium is imminent, he has a conversation with her old friend Kit. She assures him that Sue will quit her job on his return. He asks if staying home will be enough for her.

> "I don't know," Kit said honestly. "After all, that's up to her—and you."
>
> "It's up to her," Bill said.

And there, after a final scene of Bill's happy return to domestic mayhem, the matter rests.

"You Shall Hear of Me"

Lord Jim, by Joseph Conrad

s I look down the mental shelf of books that formed my taste and thinking when I was a boy, I find a tame assortment of titles almost entirely predictable by the year of my birth: in addition to such classics as *Tom Sawyer* and *The Prince and the Pauper*, *Little Women* and *Little Men*, I also read sentimental drivel along the lines of *Little Lord Fauntleroy* and *The Little Lame Prince*, books I expect must now be forgotten except by deluded grandparents. The first trend in my reading that suggests an individual taste was a fascination with books about the seafaring life, particularly pirate tales. It began, of course, with *Treasure Island*, which thrilled me in a way that no book after it was ever able to match. It shivered my timbers. Then I made my way through *Kidnapped* and *The Master of Ballantrae*, moved on to Stevenson imitations such as *Moonfleet*, by J. Meade Falkner, and *The Coral Island*, by R. M. Ballantyne, and embarked on my first voyage into nonfiction: Richard Henry Dana's *Two Years Before the Mast*, which enraptured me as much as my favorite make-believe books.

With my love of tales of the sea, I inevitably found my way to Conrad, but my discovery of his books happened early, perhaps before I was ready. I was thirteen when I read *Lord Jim*. It came to me in the guise of a gaudy paperback, published to profit from the release of a new film version starring Peter O'Toole, with a breathless blurb promising a lusty tale of adventure on a tropical isle. *Lawrence of Arabia*, which I had seen two years earlier, was my first important experience at the cinema: when I saw young O'Toole, with those soul-impaling pale blue eyes, pirouette in the desert in his Arab robes, my heart stopped, seized by the deepest throes of romantic hero worship. Richard Brooks's film version of *Lord Jim*, with O'Toole in the title role, came out a few years later. I never saw it, but I understand that it was a failure, among both the Conradians and the adventure-film set; if it came to my neighborhood theater, it was gone before I had a chance to persuade my father—a cinematophobe with a particular aversion to British accents who was still recovering from the sitting marathon of *Lawrence of Arabia*—to take me to see it. Yet flop or not, the movie had a tie-in paperback with Peter O'Toole's beautiful, enigmatic face on the cover, which grabbed me and my fifty cents.

I find it difficult to reconstruct a chronology of my reading habits with any precision; I tend to organize my memories as a reader around themes. I know exactly when I read *Lord Jim*: it was the summer of 1965, the year the movie was released. But I have no idea whether it came before or after, for example, *The Catcher in the Rye* or *A Tale of Two Cities*, two other books I read that year. Looking back on my early-adolescent reading, I see those three books as the beginnings of different long-term reading projects: Dickens, contemporary American literature, and modernism. I'm certain that when I read *Jim* for the first time, I had never heard of modernism, but I knew at once that I was encountering a book quite different from *Treasure Island* in technique and intent.

It was my first experience with ambiguity, a literary quality that Robert Louis Stevenson avoided. It also involved a much more complex delivery system than I was accustomed to. The book started off with the comforting, familiar presence of the omniscient narrator, but by the fifth chapter he was gone, replaced by someone named Marlow, who continued the tale in the form of an endless after-dinner storytelling session on the veranda of a hotel in Singapore. The description of cigar ends burning in the tropical dark made a vivid impression. Then the ending came in the form of letters from Marlow to one of the men who had listened to his monologue on the porch. It struck me that in its narrative structure, *Lord Jim* was similar to *Wuthering Heights*—the beginning of another lifelong reading project, romanticism.

I read *Lord Jim* where I read everything, lying in my bed, in a dark corner of my room, in my family's house in suburban Houston. My room was at the top of the stairs by the front door, far from where the rest of the family slept, presided over by a huge poster of *The Pirates of Penzance*. A bit of ingenuity with the pillows and the gooseneck lamp made it impossible for my mother downstairs to see if the light was on after bedtime, and the rumble of the window-mounted air conditioner gave the room exactly the same sense of coziness, in the dreadful Texas summer heat, that I would later experience by a fireplace in cold, damp places. When my parents called up to me from downstairs, always for something less interesting than my book, I could pretend not to hear them, safe in the knowledge that they wouldn't climb the stairs unless it was important. I've never found a place that was better for reading.

Lord Jim started off in the best possible way for me, with Jim's experiences at a maritime academy in England. His age isn't stated, but the narrator makes it clear he's a teenager, probably just two or three years older than I was. The boy Jim was "generally liked." He had "an excellent physique." In the evenings, he would live in his mind "the sea-life of light literature." He saw himself saving people from sinking ships, cutting away masts in a hurricane, swimming through surf with a line; or as a lonely castaway, barefooted and half-naked, walking on uncovered reefs in search of shellfish to stave off starvation. He confronted savages on tropical shores, quelled mutinies on the high seas, and in a small boat upon the ocean kept up the hearts of despairing men—always an example of devotion to duty, and as unflinching as a hero in a book.

Those were *my* daydreams: I was Jim! Needless to say, that wasn't me at all but rather the me I dreamed of being, in my imminent future life as Peter O'Toole's best friend. My physique was not excellent at all, rather painfully skinny, and although I had friends, I was too bookish to be generally liked. One of the most excruciating moments in my life had come in the school year just completed, when a boy with an excellent physique, who was generally liked, actually spoke to me—and referred to my private passion, as if he could read my mind. He asked me, in front of his friends, "Why are you a pirate's dream?" I was dazzled by the very thought of it: How could I ever be a pirate's dream? Then he painfully thumped my sternum and said, "Sunken chest!"—and walked away laughing. I burned with anguish and tragic shame as only a humiliated thirteen-year-old can do.

The story became much more complicated after Marlow took over and reconstructed Jim's act of cowardice at sea, when he abandoned his ship to save his own skin—the moment the hero flinched. I was puzzled and intermittently bored by a story in which the hero failed to do what he had dreamed of doing when he was a boy. Nonetheless, I kept reading, having already developed an aversion to setting aside a book halfway through, as Marlow pieced Jim's story together in that rambling, roundabout way of his. When I reread *Lord Jim* this year, I had an almost continuous feeling of surprise that my thirteen-year-old self had been able to wade through so much ambiguity and irony and fine moral distinction making. I must have known something about irony, because half the words that came out of my father's mouth were ironic, but I could not have understood the joke about living in the mind "the sea-life of light literature," since that was still one of the main motives of my own reading.

The second half of the book, when Jim arrives in Borneo and finally does the right thing, was much more to my taste: he had a girlfriend, which was tedious, but the mushy stuff was kept to a minimum, and the story was crammed with action. Jim and his best friend, Dain Waris, the son of the good chief, subdue their enemies and bring peace and order to the village—until the arrival of a group of white desperadoes (whom I recognized on my rereading as pirates, though Conrad doesn't call them that). I was moved by Marlow's description of Jim standing on the shore of his new home, waving farewell to his friend as he sailed away, and took to heart Jim's parting words, which seemed to me even then the defiant national anthem of adolescence: "I saw him aft detached upon the light of the westering sun, raising his cap high above his head. I heard an indistinct shout, 'You—shall—hear—of—me.'"

One of the most popular oracles in late antiquity and the Middle Ages was the *sortes Vergilianae*, in which the petitioner opened a copy of the *Aeneid* and chose a verse at random, without peeking, to predict the future. The practice was based upon the belief that Virgil's poems, like those of Homer, contained all human learning and wisdom; if the consultation gave an unreliable forecast, at least it might offer some good advice. Nowadays, if somebody says a book is magical, chances are he's trying to sell it to you. Yet every now and then a book comes along that appears to exert an uncanny influence on your life. I don't mean that in the sense that its ideas change your way of thinking, but rather "uncanny" in the old Scots sense of the word, meaning that it possesses occult powers—like the predictive ability the Romans attributed to the *Aeneid*.

As I reread my *sortes Conradensis*, the thought that kept recurring to me was how closely it had predicted my own life. On the second page, before flashing back to Jim's school days, the book describes his later career as a "water-clerk," or salesman for a ship chandler: "Thus in the course of years he was known successively in Bombay, in Calcutta, in Rangoon, in Penang, in Batavia." I reread those words sitting on the porch of my house in Jakarta—as Batavia has been known since 1949. Since my travels in Asia began sixteen years ago, I too have spent some time—been known, you might say—in those places, all except Calcutta; it's still on my "not yet" list. I have been a party to a few after-dinner storytelling sessions at hotels in Singapore, though the verandas now are usually glazed and air-conditioned. I have slept in the jungle of Borneo, in a village much like Jim's. Dain Waris is Buginese, born on the island of Celebes, now called Sulawesi, and so is my own best friend, my partner Rendy. Conrad writes of the Bugis: "The men of that race are intelligent, enterprising, revengeful, but with a more frank courage than the other Malays, and restless under oppression." The words could have been written to describe Rendy, except that as far as I know he has never exacted revenge of any sort. I'm certain that he would be restless under oppression, but since I have known him, he has refused to submit to anything like that. Conrad might have added "stubborn" to the list.

Our house in Jakarta isn't as tranquil a literary refuge as my boyhood room, though it's quite as comfortable, perpetually breezy thanks to the L-shaped garden that encloses it. It can't really be described as a quiet house; we're just around the corner from the neighborhood mosque, which broadcasts a loudly amplified call to prayer five times a day. After the predawn call on the first night we spent here, I announced at breakfast that we would have to leave the house, that I couldn't possibly live with such a racket. Ten days later, I was sleeping right through it. It's a long story why I came to live in Indonesia, revolving around certain inequities in U.S. immigration law that make it all but impossible for Rendy even to visit my country. It is in every way a tiresome subject. Suffice it to say that I grew bored with feeling bitter about my own country and decided to take up residence in his.

As I knew it would, my recent reading of *Lord Jim* turned up much that had eluded me the first time. My understanding of the concept of honor, which governs Jim's life, has changed a great deal since I first read the book. At thirteen, under the moral influence of Robert Louis Stevenson, *The Count of Monte Cristo*, and the Boy Scouts, I found it unambiguously clear that Jim lost his honor when he abandoned his ship, and regained it with his act of bravery in Borneo, resulting in his death in the last chapter. It was a quest, pure and simple, which ended as all quest stories must, in the successful attainment of the goal. My concept of honor would soon be transformed in school, when we read *Henry IV, Part 1* in English class, and I heard what Falstaff had to say on the subject. I still see honor as an essential part of a good life, and I also see it as an empty slogan used to justify all kinds of wickedness—a word, air, a mere scutcheon. And there, with Jim and Falstaff, began my catechism.

My rereading also gave me insight into the accusation, made by many critics since I first read the book, that Conrad is a racist. One of the principal moral ambiguities of the novel arises from the fact that Jim is killed not by an enemy but by a friend. The book's plot, slow to come to a boil, overflows in the last few chapters: Dain Waris's father, Doramin, the sympathetic Bugis chief who lets Jim pretty much run his village, shoots him on the last page of the book because he wrongly believes that Jim is in league with the white desperadoes responsible for Dain Waris's death. Jim knows Doramin will assume this, yet walks right up to him and his wife as they mourn over the body of their son. "Whispers followed him; murmurs: 'He has worked all the evil.' 'He hath a charm.' . . . He heard them—perhaps!" The old man picks up a gun and shoots Jim. "They say that the white man sent right and left at all those faces a proud and unflinching glance. Then with his hands over his lips he fell forward, dead."

In order for the ending to make sense, the reader must accept the assumption, vaguely hinted at and never justified, that Doramin, despite his years of friendship with Jim, is incapable of dissociating him from the evil white men who killed his son. Doramin isn't evil himself; he's simply not endowed with the powers of ratiocination that would enable him to make such a distinction, and he has an impulsive, brutish nature that disposes him to kill without hesitation. (Hence the foreshadowing that the Bugis are vengeful people.) I generally detest criticizing literature through the lens of contemporary morality, yet at the same time I find that most people who gripe about "political correctness" have a hidden agenda to whisk us back to a mythical golden age, when life was simpler and no one complained (and, as it happened, people who looked just like them ran the world). My principal objection to the denouement of *Lord Jim*, which comes early in Conrad's career as a writer, is that it's lazy, relying on the imperialist cliché of the violent, irrational savage—one that was familiar to the readers of *Blackwood's Magazine*, where the tale was first published. I don't doubt that someone like Doramin might have concluded that Jim was in league with the desperadoes, and might have made such a calculation based on the fact that he was white; but when the author expects me to take that assumption for granted, based upon my experience as a reader of "light literature"— what we now call genre fiction—rather than on his narrative of events and his presentation of the characters, then his book itself becomes light literature.

Indonesia is an endlessly fascinating country, as big and diverse and rich in its way as the United States. I've learned a lot by living here, about the country and its way of life, its arts and religions. The experience has also taught me that you can live anywhere. When I first moved to Indonesia, my friends in New York, where I had spent more than twenty years, joked that I wouldn't last long without Western theater and opera and art museums. Yet the life of the mind respects no national boundaries. Just as the boy Jim performed picturesque acts of heroism in his imagination, so I find few limits here on where I can go and what I can do. (I concede that it's been even easier since I got broadband Internet access.) I have made many friends: some are Indonesians, but most are other expatriates, mainly because my command of Indonesian (not to mention Javanese and Bugis) is shaky. Expatriates are generally good company: people who choose to live in faraway places, where they do everything differently from how they do it at home, are necessarily imaginative and broad-minded.

When I read *Lord Jim* the second time around, more important than the heightened sophistication of my literary analysis was my discovery that one of Conrad's central themes is the strange life of the expatriate. He was one himself, of course: when he was seventeen, Józef Teodor Konrad Korzeniowski left his native Poland to follow the sea, and he never lived there again. Critics (rightly, in my view) have elevated him to the upper ether of the literary pantheon for his exploration of the themes of alienation and futility and man's propensity for evil. But he wasn't dealing with these themes in a general way, even if the moral dilemmas of his most complex characters have a universal application. No, in his finest novels he wrote about the particular forms of spiritual unease experienced by expatriates: the alienation of idealistic cosmopolites such as the Goulds and Dr. Monygham in *Nostromo*, and the futility of that book's eponymous hero, an Italian in South America. In *The Secret Agent*, Mr. Verloc, a Russian living in London, presides over a veritable nest of expatriates in the upstairs room of his shop. Kurtz is as far from home as a man can be. Unlike the seafarer Marlow—Conrad's storytelling mouthpiece, his genial chorus, who dreams of retiring to England—the central characters in the novels aren't wanderers; they are foreigners who, like me, have found a place to stay. Like their creator, they are not simply alienated; they are aliens.

When Marlow visits Jim in Borneo, he meets Doramin and his "little, motherly witch of a wife." Doramin tells him that Jim, like all white men, will leave them someday. Marlow seeks to reassure him, insisting that Jim is different. Then the old woman speaks from behind her peephole of purdah: "Without removing her eyes from the vast prospect of forests stretching as far as the hills, she asked me in a pitying voice why was it that he so young had wandered from his home, coming so far, through so many dangers? Had he no household there, no kinsmen in his own country? Had he no old mother, who would always remember his face?" As I read the book on my porch, in a deepening dusk that vibrated with the plangent call to prayer from the mosque, Jim came fully alive for me for the first time when I saw him through the sentimental eyes of Dain Waris's mother. I thought of my mother, and my father, my kinsmen in my own country, who will always remember my face. Then I really was Jim.

Love with a Capital L

The Vagabond and *The Shackle*, by Colette

hen I was in my twenties, my friends and I read Colette as others read the Bible. She was our Book of Wisdom. We read her for solace, and for moral instruction. We read her to learn better who we were, and how, given the constraint of our condition, we were to live. The condition, of course, was that we were women, and that Love (as we had all long known) was the territory upon which our battle with Life was to be pitched. Not another living writer, it seemed to us, understood the situation as well as Colette. No one, in fact, came close. She alone had stared long and hard into the heart of the matter. In her work we could see ourselves not only as we were but as we were likely to become. It was the *potential* for self-recognition that made Colette's novels so compelling.

It was a tricky business, loving Colette as we did, one that spoke to acute inner dividedness. We were intellectually in- clined girls, English majors whose relation to literature was high-minded, romantic, amateurish. On the one hand, we read Henry James and George Eliot only to imagine ourselves as Isabel Archer or Dorothea Brooke, passionately intelligent young women destined for pedestrian tragedy at the hands of famously unworthy men. On the other, we were daily absorbed by a hungry fantasy of ourselves as new women, literary and independent; in this spirit we read Mary McCarthy. *The Company She Keeps* gave us back a female protagonist in whom we could see ourselves reflected as we actually were, right then and there (Oh god! we moaned over "The Man in the Brooks Brothers Shirt," that is *just* the way it is). McCarthy's central character was a budding "free" woman whose sexual humiliations were redeemed for us through the delicious brilliance of a prose edged in glittering irony and leveled at those who held the power. What fools her men were, mean and pathetic. Just to see them so portrayed, lowered into a bath of scorn, was to feel ourselves raised up. That, of course, was the thing with McCarthy, the scorn: scorn applied as balm against the surface of the wound.

Yet McCarthy's scorn had, ultimately, the power neither to penetrate nor to clarify. What she knew wasn't sufficient; didn't go far enough, deep enough, something enough. It only brought us back to Colette—this modern bohemian of two generations ago—whose writing achieved so much nuance, so much quick-paced change, such fluidity of thought and feeling that, in her hands, being swamped by sexual attraction had the power of metaphor. Colette's work sounded depths of understanding that were like nothing we had ever encountered. She seemed to know everything that *actually* went on inside a woman "in the grip." Her wisdom riveted your eyes to the page, gathered up your scattered, racing inattention. It made A Woman in Love as serious a concern for the novelist as God or War. As you read on in Colette, the noise within died down; at the center, stillness and silence began to gather; a point of entry into the human condition was about to be reached.

Two novels became imprinted on me: *The Vagabond* and *The Shackle*. In these books Colette dramatized the "condition" in a voice more nakedly autobiographical than any she would ever again assume. Here we found a glamorous loneliness, the kind we fantasized as emblematic of the contemporary woman who need no longer absorb in Victorian silence the slings and arrows of outrageous married fortune. She was free now to pick up and go. . . . And then what? Colette would tell us.

For years I had by heart the following passage from *The Vagabond*:

> Behold me then, just as I am! This evening I shall not be able to escape the meeting in the long mirror, the soliloquy which I have a hundred times avoided, accepted, fled from, taken up again and broken off. I feel in advance, alas, the uselessness of trying to change the subject. This evening I shall not feel sleepy, and the spell of a book — even a brand-new book with that smell of printers' ink and paper fresh from the press that makes you think of coal and trains and departures!—even that spell will not be able to distract me from myself.
>
> Behold me then, just as I am! Alone, alone, and for the rest of my life, no doubt.

Alone! Really one might think I was pitying myself for it!

"If you live all alone," [says a friend,] "it's because you really want to, isn't it?"

Certainly I "really" want to, and in fact I *want* to, quite simply. Only, well . . . there are days when solitude, for someone of my age, is a heady wine which intoxicates you with freedom, others when it is a poison which makes you beat your head against the wall.

How we resonated at twenty-three to this situation—and to think, it was being lived at a time when a new book in one's hands could remind the reader of coal, trains, and departure! Renée Néré, the astonishingly forthright narrator of *The Vagabond* and *The Shackle*, is a woman in her thirties whose fractured identity is central to her existence. She has written books, she has divorced her husband, she has gone on the stage. And now, here she is suffering the consequences of her actions.

Yet Renée's hold on her newfound independence is transparently shaky (even we could see that). Take, for instance, the curious business of her writing. Although she has published two books, writing is a fugitive longing in Renée. Why? The impulse, quite simply, is not strong enough:

From time to time I feel a need, sharp as thirst in summer, to note and to describe. . . . The attack does not last long; it is but the itching of an old scar. . . . It takes up too much time to write. And the trouble is, I am no Balzac! The fragile story I am constructing crumbles away when the tradesman rings, or the shoemaker sends in his bill, when the solicitor, or one's counsel, telephones, or when the theatrical agent summons me to his office.

Hardly the words of one compelled by her talent to make art (again, a situation we understood *perfectly*). The desire in a woman to be "free" is (we well knew) easily undermined by desire itself. Struggle as she may, a woman is always torn between the longing for independence and the need for love. It is this, really—the Question of Love—that, as we soon saw, commands Renée's real attention. Love has come, and love has gone. Should it come again, she muses repeatedly, will she give in to the siren song or will she resist with all her might? She knows everything there is to know about the emotional slavery that accompanies desire—the longings, the anxieties, the humiliations. Still, the lure is powerful.

The argument with herself about whether or not to resist love is the remarkably sustained subject of the two novels that Renée Néré narrates. In *The Vagabond* she will renounce it, in *The Shackle* she will knuckle under to it. The first gratified us, the second shocked us. Either way, we were in thrall. What carried the day was the significance, in Colette's hands, of erotic obsession. Love with a capital *L*, in both books, is the glory and the despair, equally, of a woman's life. "What torments you've thrust me into all over again," Renée cries to the friend who introduces her to the first lover. "Torments," she adds reverently, "that I wouldn't exchange for all the greatest joys." Love is the divine stigma, the extraordinary mark of a knowing life, upon which Colette's unique powers of observation were here trained.

Recently, I read these books again for the first time in more than thirty years, and the experience was unsettling. The wholly unexpected occurred: I came away from them with mixed feelings. This time around I found myself thinking, Ah yes! how brilliantly it is all evoked—the endless fantasizing, the pathological insecurity, the emptiness inside the protagonist that opens wide to take in Love with a capital *L*. Really, the writing is incomparable. But what appalling *strangers* these people are to one another! Not a speck of reality between them. How preoccupied she is with aging. Why hadn't I noticed *that* before? And the aimlessness of them all, women and men alike—especially in *The Shackle*. No one has anything to do but lie around brooding about love.

Most striking, for me—the single greatest change, in fact, in my feeling about these novels—was the sense I had that everything was taking place in a vacuum. When I had read Colette before, the world seemed to collect around the narrator's wisdom. Now I saw that Renée's reflections led back—only and always—into the secret, silent self. She was alone in the world; alone and lonely.

Early in *The Vagabond* she observes Max, her future lover, and she thinks:

> How is it that he, who is in love with me, is not in the least disturbed that he knows me so little? He clearly never gives that a thought . . . [never] does he show any eagerness to find out what I am like, to question me or read my character, and I notice that he pays more attention to the play of light on my hair than to what I am saying. . . . How strange all that is! There he sits close to me . . . [but he] is not there, he is a thousand

leagues away! I keep wanting to get up and say to him: "Why are you here? Go away!" And I do nothing of the kind. . . . Does he think? Does he read? Does he work? I believe he belongs to that large rather commonplace class of persons who are interested in everything and do absolutely nothing. Not a trace of wit, a certain quickness of comprehension, a very adequate vocabulary enhanced by a beautiful rich voice, that readiness to laugh with a childish gaiety that one sees in many men—such is my admirer.

The absence of connection between them is penetrating—and unabating. Four years later, in *The Shackle*, Renée, now retired from the stage and openly at loose ends, falls into an affair with Jean, a man she could describe much as she did Max, and one with whom the association is even more nakedly chemical—and isolating:

Our honest bodies have clung together with a mutual thrill of delight they will remember the next time they touch, while our souls will withdraw again behind the barrier of the same dishonest but expedient silence. . . . We had learnt already that . . . [e]mbracing gives us the illusion of being united and silence makes us believe we are at peace. . . . I have insulted this lover . . . by giving him my body and supposing that this was enough. He has returned the insult . . . for nothing is exchanged in the sexual act. . . . [O]ur love which had begun in silence and the sexual act was ending in the sexual act and silence.

This is the anxiety of infatuation speaking—Colette at her absolute best—the anxiety of knowing that one is not known, that one is (marvelously, terribly) only a catalyst for another's desire. This anxiety is the thing Colette knows through and through: the wisdom at the heart of her fame, there, from the beginning, like a smoking gun; the source, inevitably, of her narrator's obsessive preoccupation with aging.

In the earliest pages of *The Vagabond*, Renée stares pitilessly into the mirror. She is thirty-three years old, and the dreaded decline is eating at her. If it weren't for that, she might stay with Max after all, even though she can't talk to him. But at the end, when he proposes marriage, promising lifelong happiness and security, she breaks off the affair with a letter of explanation that says it all:

> I am no longer a young woman. . . . Imagine me [in a few years' time], still beautiful but desperate, frantic in my armour of corset and frock, under my make-up and powder . . . beautiful as a full-blown rose which one must not touch. A glance of yours, resting on a young woman, will be enough to lengthen the sad crease that smiling has engraved on my cheek, but a happy night in your arms will cost my fading beauty dearer still. . . . What this letter lacks is . . . all the thoughts I am hiding from you, the thoughts that have been poisoning me for so long. . . . Ah! How young you are. Your hell is limited to not possessing what you desire, a thing which some people have to put up with all their lives. But to possess what one loves and every minute to feel one's sole treasure disintegrating, melting, and slipping away like gold dust between one's fingers! And not to have the dreadful courage to open one's hand and let the whole treasure go, but to clench one's fingers ever tighter, and to cry and beg to keep . . . what? a precious little trace of gold in the hollow of one's palm.

Who but Colette could have etched this portrait (acid on zinc) of a woman staring into the hell that seems reserved

for women alone? And who but Colette could have failed so
entirely to unpack it?

When I read Colette in my twenties, I said to myself, That is
exactly the way it is. Now I read her and I find myself thinking, How much smaller this all seems than it once did—cold,
brilliant, limited—and silently I am saying to her, Why
aren't you making more sense of things? Yes, I have from
you the incomparable feel of an intelligent woman in the
grip of romantic obsession, and that is strong stuff. But sexual passion as a driving force doesn't seem to matter on its
own, as it once did. It no longer feels large. Certainly, it no
longer feels metaphoric.

Why? I ask myself. Is it that I no longer "identify" with
the delicious despair of erotic love? Hardly. I have learned
over a long enough life that at any moment anyone who is
alive can feel it all—the joy, the panic, the sick excitement—
exactly as she did at twenty-five or thirty-five. No, it is a matter not of feeling but of altered sensibility: not only mine but
that of the culture as well. The question to ask is, Does a person who is twenty-five today read Colette as *I* read her at
twenty-five? And the answer to that, I'm afraid, is also:
hardly. It's not that *I* have passed from youth to middle age,
it's that the culture has undergone a sea change. Even though
we *feel* love as we always did, we don't *make* of it what we
once did.

When *The Vagabond* was published in 1910, André Gide
sent Colette a letter of extravagant admiration: he thought

the novel brilliant and powerful. For the next forty years, Colette's work would be received in the same spirit by every leading literary light throughout Europe and America. She was beloved not only for her mastery of the French language—her famous style—but also because she said things that struck a nerve deep in the culture. Her books persuaded her readers that something fundamental and immutable was being described: naked, unadorned, and irreducibly true. It is impossible to imagine the same response being accorded this work today—not because it is about love (Tolstoy, Flaubert, and Stendhal are also about love), but because it is *only* about love.

So where does that leave me? Filled with righteous feminist rejection of Colette? Not so easy as that. I walk around these days feeling as though pieces of her writing lie heavy on my chest. Sometimes a sentence lifts itself off the surface, and stands in the air before me. . . . "Our honest bodies [cling] together with a mutual thrill of delight . . . while our souls . . . withdraw again behind the barrier." Repeatedly, I lean in toward the prose. Then, of course, that which has changed in me shrinks, holds back, stiffens. I *want* the reading of Colette to be the same as it once was, but it is not. Yet I am wrenched by the beauty of that which no longer feels large, and can never feel large again.

Stead Made Me Do It

House of All Nations, **by Christina Stead**

he phone call would come at 3:00 a.m., and the town car would materialize fifteen minutes later: a sleek and murmurous vehicle that was a most unlikely sight on my Brooklyn side street. The backseat was as soft as the bed I had just abandoned, and the route the uniformed driver followed was always the same: through downtown Brooklyn, over the Brooklyn Bridge, into the financial district.

One night stands out from the rest.

The driver this time was an older man, an Eastern European émigré who spoke hardly any English. As we rounded the corner of Fourth and Atlantic, I saw a trio of figures struggling under a streetlamp. A woman in a bronze minidress and platform heels swung a trapezoid-shaped handbag to fend off two assailants wearing the 1980s equivalent of zoot suits. I was half-dead with sleep and there seemed no way to focus on the sights cordoned off by the window. They demanded response, didn't they?

But no, they had already floated past.

To the driver I said, "I think she was having trouble."

He muttered unintelligibly.

"Don't you have a radio or something—to call the police?"

"No radio."

We were on the bridge approach by now—and then on the bridge itself. In the near distance was a cliff wall of lights.

Finally, devolving into the narrow backstreets of lower Manhattan, we arrived at our destination: the financial printing firm where I had worked for the previous two years. It was here that I typed in the last-minute edits that lawyers cubbyholed elsewhere in the building made on business documents about to be filed with the Securities and Exchange Commission in Washington, D.C.

Up the elevator. Into the composition room. Instructions came from my colleague Alba, who had already done four hours of overtime and had a car downstairs waiting to take her home to Queens: "It's lighter now, but they're still making changes. You'll have to watch for page runs."

A go-between came in with the latest page proofs for a People Express annual report.

Call the police? But that was ten minutes ago, in another dimension.

People Express was not doing well. People Express was selling another airplane in order to meet its interest payments.

There was a particular reason I had taken this job, and it was a literary reason. Nine years earlier, as a bookstore clerk in North Carolina, I had come across a novel on the remainder tables that impressed me with its heft and enticed me with its title: *House of All Nations*. The author was Christina Stead, an Australian who lived in Paris from 1929 to 1935, working in a bank there.

In 1976, I was twenty-two years old, with a peripatetic childhood behind me (England, Holland, New Jersey) and an admiration for the ironic and the cosmopolitan in fiction, as well as for the lyrical, the gothic, the unhinged. *House of All Nations*, it turned out, would come through on all counts—but I didn't know that yet. Instead, it was the gorgeous Gilbert Stone jacket art on the 1972 reissue that initially caught my eye. It showed a shadowy, bowler-hatted banker and, behind him, a somber mausoleum of granite and gold. The novel's eight hundred closely printed pages also exuded an appeal, making a sumptuous flopping sound as I thumbed through them. And then there were the rambunctious titles of the book's 104 "scenes" (Stead's preference over "chapters"): "He Travels Fast But Not Alone," "Whoopee Party," "The Man with Cunard-Colored Eyes," "No Money in Working for a Living." How could I resist?

I bought the book, took it to the beach, and quickly came to a realization: I lacked the wherewithal to read it. The early specialization of my British high-school and university

education meant I had never had the slightest brush with finance, and all the novel's fiscal wheeling and dealing went
way over my head. What, in this context, did "put" and "call"
mean, or "long" and "short"? What exactly were "margins"
and "options"?

Yet the characters' money talk was mesmerizing—for even
though they all dealt in the same arcane vocabulary, each
used it differently, revealing different rhythms of mind,
quirks of temperament, degrees of paranoia, frenzies of
power hunger. Besides, it wasn't all business. South American
playboys, cynical countesses, quixotic Communists, scheming harridans, and blackmailing drug fiends all played roles,
whether major or minor, in this jittery portrait of sleazy
Parisian bankers making money off the Crash. Perhaps that
was what kept me reading, for I loved fiction with a vivid
sense of history—and *House of All Nations*, set in 1931–32,
made you feel you were *there*, riding the downward spiral of
economic collapse, buffeted by billowing war clouds each step
of the way.

Other fiction I had read or was soon to read—Ford Madox
Ford's *Parade's End*, Günter Grass's *The Tin Drum*, Elsa
Morante's *History: A Novel*—had given me my sense of a
Europe defined by war. But nothing else had zeroed in so
closely on between-wars queasiness. Why had I only vaguely
heard of Stead? Why was *The Man Who Loved Children* the
one book repeatedly named as her masterpiece? How could
anyone relegate *House of All Nations*—a novel that chews
up and spits out the spirit of a whole decade—to ancillary
status in the Stead canon?

I was overreacting. *House of All Nations* is generally ranked a close second to Stead's best-known novel. Still, when I went on to read *The Man Who Loved Children* in order to make the comparison for myself, it disappointed me even as I acknowledged its brute force. It seemed merely human, whereas *House* was diabolic. *The Man Who Loved Children* portrayed familiar territory: family misery. *House* entered realms and harnessed writerly powers I could only begin to imagine.

And there was this too: Stead, a writer sometimes saddled with the label "feminist," wrote more knowingly and incisively about businessmen than any other writer, male or female, I had ever encountered.

In 1979, I moved from North Carolina to New York, and in 1980 my first novel was accepted in two weeks flat. That same spring, in the space of three months, I wrote a rough draft for a second book I liked much better, a workplace tale, written under Henry Green's influence as much as Stead's. It would take five years to place. Nothing much happened with either novel. I was still working in bookstores.

In 1983, Christina Stead died at age eighty. I had the flu that week, and when I called in sick, one of my fellow clerks, knowing I was a Stead fan, assumed this was just my excuse to stay home and mourn. That was also the year I realized that if I didn't start making more money soon, I wouldn't be able to survive the city's skyrocketing rents.

I took a word-processing course and became, briefly, an

"administrative assistant" (in other words, a secretary). Then a typesetting job at R. R. Donnelley's financial printing division opened up and I took it. I had heard we were living in a speculation-crazed decade, and this seemed my chance to observe it firsthand. I knew I lacked a head for numbers, but I thought that frequent handling of business documents might help me to develop one—whereupon I could write my own novel about finance and become the Christina Stead of the 1980s.

Because most documents were fine-tuned overnight for filing with the SEC the next morning, I worked crazy hours—usually 4:00 p.m. to midnight. Even on day shift, there was a chance that I'd be asked to come in early—hence the 3:00 a.m. phone calls.

I saw lots of documents. I was required to sign oaths promising that I would not take advantage of my insider's access to do any insider trading. I signed—and despaired. The idea of my doing insider trading was laughable. Apart from the obvious death-throe symptoms of People Express, nothing registered. I began to grow quite fond of certain typefaces and I liked doing layout for cover pages, but the *content* of what I was typing was mind-numbing.

Nevertheless, some Stead-like local color came with the job. During another one of my "3:00 a.m. specials" (as I began to think of them), the car-service driver voiced his worries to me, saying he knew full well he was shipping drugs along with documents to legal types up and down the town, but he didn't know whether to believe his bosses when they told him he was in no danger of being arrested if caught. (Arrangements had been made, they said.) And once, during a lull in office activity, a colleague and I had fun trading information on who in the office did cocaine ("But he's a health nut!") and who was gay ("But he's a nice Italian boy!").

So far, so good. There was rumored drug use in *House of All Nations*—and at least one homosexual.

On another night, an envelope addressed to a customer service representative turned out to be full of white powder. A receptionist, thinking the package contained page proofs, had opened it. The addressee was fired, and we worried terribly over how he would pay for his new house and new baby.

No problem: he was hired by a competitor the very next week. The utter lack of consequences was in perfect keeping with Stead.

None of this helped me with my central problem, however—that I was simply too stupid to discern the action cloaked in the language of the blue-sky memorandums and prospectuses that passed through my hands.

In the end, I thoroughly messed up my finance-novel research by quitting my job a full year before the 1987 Black Monday crash. Stead, perhaps jealously guarding her turf from beyond the grave, took some of the blame here, for while visiting Seattle in 1985, I had come across a copy of her posthumous collection, *Ocean of Story*, at the Elliott Bay Book Company. The book was nowhere to be found in any of the cramped New York bookstores I frequented—and so, partly on the strength of this, I moved out West in 1986.

I had all Stead's published books in my library by then,

but had begun to realize I could never meaningfully emulate her. In fact, I had given up trying to understand even my own paltry finances. At tax time, I turned everything over to an accountant.

I review books on a weekly basis, so the ultimate luxury—one I am unable to indulge in very often—is to reread: to revisit a book to see how time has treated it, how memory has distorted it, or how my own passing years have cast a new light on it.

It was an odd sensation, more than two decades after first encountering *House of All Nations*, to look again at a book that had shaped me in such serious and absurd ways, for it unerringly revealed how much one can't know, or can't remember, about one's own reading and writing.

There were minor things, such as the carnival festivity of Stead's vocabulary: words like "canoodle" and "tatterdemalion." Could I first have come across them here? I've certainly used them since, in ways that begin to feel uncomfortably derivative. Or punctuation: I thought I got my exclamation points from Paul Theroux! But, no, they're here too—so perhaps Stead's punctuation whetted an appetite that Theroux merely continued to satisfy.

On a deeper level, Stead's work has an appealingly amoral aesthetic that I now see must have been a revelation to me when I first read it. Henry James may have paved the way here, for I remember my relief when I read him at nineteen and realized how little use he had for "lessons," how purely he focused on the dynamics of the psyche and of social situations. But James is a meticulous analyst, while Stead presents her characters almost without comment. Instead, she simply lets them announce themselves, reveal themselves, and, as often as not, sink themselves. In a 1982 interview, she explained:

> I'm interested in people here and now. I have not even any moral views. Maybe, within myself I think "You shouldn't do that," but I would never write such a thing, or express it openly, because I was brought up by a naturalist [her father, David Stead], and you don't say to a snail, "You bad snail, you mustn't cross my garden path" or anything, do you? A snail crosses your garden path and he leaves a little silver trail, which is very nice of him, and it's very pretty and that's all. A sea-anemone puts out its beautiful little tentacles making it look like a flower and it catches things out of the water and eats them. You don't say, "You bad sea-anemone, you shouldn't eat those live things," do you? They *do* eat them and otherwise they wouldn't be alive and be like a lovely little flower.

In *House of All Nations*, it is this very lack of judgment that, in collusion with her giddy, caustic humor, allows Stead to probe so deeply. The book may feel like an indictment, but it's not an indictment of particular characters—it's an indictment of a society in economic anarchy that is heading inexorably toward war. Her characters, as they see it, are just making the best of a bad hand.

The sheer number of those characters—the 1938 edition supplies a cast list of more than 130—is crucial to the novel's method and moral outlook. Hazel Rowley, in her admirable *Christina Stead: A Biography*, cites a lecture that Stead gave on "the many-charactered novel" in June 1939, one year after *House of All Nations* was published. Rowley writes:

> Stead suggested that this was the ideal form of novel for a
> world in chaos in which the individual felt small. No writer
> could take sides when dealing with such a large array of char
> acters: the writer "is in the position of an impartial, disabused
> and merry god" and the reader has to "draw his own conclu
> sions from the diverse material, as from life itself."

It is this sense of having to draw your own conclusions
that, to my mind, makes *House of All Nations* more satisfying than *The Man Who Loved Children*, where you know exactly whom you're rooting for: the put-upon housewife, the
gifted but dowdy adolescent daughter.

There is also this difference between *The Man Who
Loved Children* and *House of All Nations*: the former explores subject matter that was foisted on Stead by her own
troubled girlhood, while the latter explores subject matter
that, in a bid for freedom, she sought out.

In March of 1928, Christina Stead, twenty-five years old and
filled with writerly aspirations, left her native Australia for
England. Two months later, she walked into the London offices of Strauss & Co., a grain exchange business, and was
hired as a secretary by its investment manager, William Blech,
an American of German Jewish origin—and a Marxist to boot.
By February of 1929, the two had become lovers. (Blech,
married, would take twenty-three years to obtain a divorce

from his first wife before marrying Stead in 1952.) That same month the couple moved to Paris, where both worked for a private American firm known as the Travelers' Bank, the creation of a charismatic American Army Air Service veteran, Bertrand Coles Neidecker. By 1931, Stead was making business trips to London for Neidecker and had her own "plushly furnished" office in the bank. Her job duties were vaguely defined and left plenty of time for fiction writing. She was also in an ideal position for a novelist: that of a fly on the wall.

That year, of course, was not a good one for banking. But Neidecker, with his charm, and Blech, with his hard work, managed to keep the bank afloat in perilous circumstances for another four years. In July of 1935, Neidecker skedaddled to New York, where he was arrested for fraud, and the bank was closed. Blech, who had resigned in May, was nevertheless implicated in the affair and also ended up in New York—with Stead and his mother in tow. Neidecker was subsequently freed on bail until the trial. Stead met with him in October and asked permission to write a novel about the Travelers' Bank. He gave her his blessing to write "everything she knew," Rowley tells us. "He probably never imagined that she knew as much as she did."

Stead proceeded with relish. In June of 1936 a business venture of Blech's took the couple to Spain, where she commenced writing. In mid-July, the Spanish Civil War broke out, and Stead and Blech were on the run: first to Antwerp, then to London. By October, Stead had submitted a draft to her publisher, and by the summer of 1937 she had completed her revisions. In the meantime, she and Blech had left London for southern France, before giving up on Europe altogether and heading back to New York.

Appalling conditions under which to write a novel—or were they? The tinderbox existence Stead and Blech were leading, with its multiple threats of lawsuits and war, seems only to have heightened the blend of bedlam and tension that crackles on the pages of *House of All Nations*.

In the novel, the Travelers' Bank becomes the Banque Mercure; Bertrand Coles Neidecker becomes Jules Simla Bertillon, a "hummingbird of rumor, fancy, and adventures"; and William Blech becomes Michel Alphendéry, Jules's right-hand man, an Alsatian Jew with a gift for moneymaking and a yearning to commit all his energies to the Communist Party as soon as he has steered Jules into calmer financial waters.

A host of characters swarms around this central pair, the most memorable of them being Henri Léon, a Romanianborn grain merchant. Jewish, promiscuous, and wildly inarticulate (one of his fractured monologues is described as an "elliptic hurricane"), Léon turns out to have a heart almost as big as Alphendéry's. His outline of his brilliantly profitable and strangely altruistic "wheat schematism"—which will give Yankee capitalism a much-needed shot in the arm *and* help Soviet Russia carry out its latest five-year plan—is one of the book's high points.

Undoubtedly it was the exuberant cynicism of this and other set pieces that appealed to me when I first read the novel. But there's more here than easy skepticism to appeal to a young reader—for a shimmering veil of myth plays over the nitty-gritty of greed and blackmail, especially in the depiction of Jules and the bank. Jules is, variously, superstitious and hardheaded, debonair and tantrum-prone. He is "slender, arch, and very beautiful," in the eyes of one bank employee. "'Tis pity he's a banker," says another. "He's only made to be a flier, a dancer—a messenger of the gods." Jules's own estimate of himself: "I'm just a gilded pickpocket and, believe me, a pickpocket has to have twinkling ankles."

In other words, he's an incarnation of wing-footed Mercury, the god who lends the bank its name. There seem to be no limits to the facets of his character, from the quibbling wisecracker ("What's the use of being rich if you can't be crazy?") to the driven *directeur* on the verge of a nervous breakdown ("I want highflying cash, beautiful cash, in platoons, in platoons, zooming; I want it big, rich, and plentiful, and all mine"). This, with more than four hundred pages still to go!

Jules, while vivid, isn't solid: "He took out his hat and coat and wrapped himself elegantly in them. He always had the curious appearance of being less material than the rest of mankind, part of him seemed always to belong to the chiaroscuro of a room, to the dark substance of lampposts in a street. When he moved amongst the pillars downstairs it was almost impossible to see him clearly." The bank is no less spectral. It's a "confidence trick," Jules frankly admits. Alphendéry puts it more poetically, seeing it as a "phantom bank" and, later, as a "strange palace of illusion, temptation, and beauty."

The periodic threats posed to Jules and Alphendéry by stock-market fluctuations, parisitical "friends" of the bank, and Jules's own erratic behavior sustain the tension over a remarkably prolonged narrative. Rowley tells us that Stead's editor wanted trims in the novel, and in certain scenes one can see his point. An early chapter on Alphendéry's Communist circle reads opaquely, even though its rhetoric is undercut by Alphendéry's own wryly voiced deprecation of spouted dogma. (By contrast, a later scene set in the same milieu, in which Alphendéry teaches a night class on economics to exhausted and Depression-bewildered factory workers, is deeply moving.)

Elsewhere, two paragraphs of untranslated French and German ring alarm bells, since these characters have been doing quite well, thank you, speaking an English that sounds Latinate or Teutonic, as required. But if 30 or 40 pages out of 787 don't work, who can complain? Jules's tirades may seem repetitious, but their cumulative impact is needed to give a full picture of him as he is in turn humored, chided, lambasted, and, by the end of the book, fondly remembered.

A second reading confirms how well assembled the book is, how deftly Stead juggles her vast cast and her many narrative strands, and how clearly she keeps a subplot's pivotal details before the reader over a stretch of five hundred pages or more. A second reading also reveals a vein of the book that somehow escaped my notice the first time around, or else had faded from memory: the finely shaded and loving tribute it pays to European and Levantine Jewry. Stead was a third-generation atheist of Protestant extraction, but her devotion to Blech was instrumental here. As Rowley puts it, "Blech was proud of his Jewishness; so was Stead." More than half the main characters in *House* are Jewish, and they compose a rich mosaic of personalities and types—some rascally, some generous, some observers of their faith, others ebulliently cynical.

Everywhere there is a sense that an intrinsic part of European character is being squeezed into an impossible corner. Stead had no way of imagining the particulars of the death-camp horrors in store. Yet she, like her characters, sensed something awful, just over the horizon, with a conviction approaching clairvoyance.

Mixed in with this salute to a roaming, cosmopolitan Jewish culture is Stead's palpable love for Michel Alphendéry—a reflection, no doubt, of her love for William Blech. Alphendéry lends the book a warmth that spills over into many of its characters, despite their shenanigans. Only one other portrait in Stead's fiction is so affectionate: that of Edward Massine in *The People with the Dogs*, another man-about-town deeply divided in nature—not between political credo and personal loyalty, but between general love of his fellow creatures and fear of a particular romantic commitment. (It may be worth noting here that the distinguishing characteristic of Stead villains and villainesses is not their evil intentions but their utterly *undivided* natures—a delusional certainty of self that prevents them from questioning their actions, no matter how transparently destructive those actions might be.)

A last, minor point: How, the first time around, could I have missed the distinctly homoerotic terms in which these wheelers and dealers' scheming and subterfuges are described? If ever a writer pinpointed the way a businessman of a certain type sees women as merely decorative and discardable, while male colleagues embody the central passion of his life, it is Stead. True, this can be seen as standard business-world misogyny, but there's something else going on here. Midway through the book, for instance, a millionaire's henchman named Davigdor Schicklgrüber—a self-proclaimed idiot who is cannier than he admits about the money he handles— traipses through Paris banking circles, and the author has maximum fun with him: "No athletic beauty married to an invalid, no youth of sixteen, no debonair valetudinarian in a low vaudeville show, no dowager in pink organdie at Nice, ever felt the desires that rich men felt when Davigdor passed their way."

This lust for Davigdor, admittedly, approaches burlesque. But the wayward beauty of Jules repeatedly enchants the book's male characters as often as the female, and works on the reader too as one of the key lures of the novel.

One benefit of learning your own limits as a writer is reaching the point where, in reading a book, you recognize straight off that you can't make use of it—so you simply sit back and savor an author who, like an acrobat or a silversmith or a high-C soprano, does things you will never, with all the training and practice in the world, be able to do.

Clearly, *House of All Nations* does plenty of things I'll never be able to do. For a start, it catches me up passionately in a subject matter that, on the surface, I have no interest in as a reader and no talent for as a writer. (Surely this is one definition of a great book.) It shows me that in the right hands, even the most unpromising topics—wheat shipments, letters of credit—can give rise to fictional wizardry.

For the longest time, I have to admit, the book misled me. It was a holy grail, a talisman, a reference point, and I embraced it the same way I've stepped aboard the wrong train, eager to begin my journey but headed in the wrong direction. I remain in awe of *House of All Nations*, knowing I'm not likely to pull off anything like it.

But after all, there's no need; it's already been done.

Pemberley Previsited

Pride and Prejudice, by Jane Austen

he first time I read *Pride and Prejudice* I was nine. I was a pert, excitable, giggly reader. My school librarian couldn't stand me. She had already spoken to me about saving books for when you were older, and suggested ominously that the novel would be ruined for me later on. "Someday," she predicted, "you're going to get too big for your britches."

I'm sure she wouldn't have let me take the novel out of her library, but of course it didn't come from her shelves. I'd found it at the University of Hawaii. My mother was the chair of women's studies there, and my sister and I spent hours after school in the small program library with the books by women authors, the anthropological studies, and, particularly, the variorum edition of *Wonder Woman*. I knew my mother loved Jane Austen, so when I came upon *Pride and Prejudice*, I curled up on a couple of floor cushions in the lounge and began to read.

My school librarian was not entirely wrong. There was a good deal in the book I was too young to understand. I skipped over hard words and long epistolary passages. Nuances of character and the delicate mechanics of plot were lost on me. Like a water insect I skated the surface of the text, scarcely dimpling the rippling current underneath. But I do remember laughing as I read. "Come here, child," Mr. Bennet tells Elizabeth, after her mother orders her to reconsider the odiously officious Mr. Collins. "An unhappy alternative is before you. . . . From this day you must be a stranger to one of your parents. Your mother will never see you again if you do *not* marry Mr. Collins, and I will never see you again if you *do*." I understood that wry proposition perfectly. If nothing else, Austen's buoyant wit came through.

The second time I read the book I was in high school and taking a summer English course that sandwiched *Pride and Prejudice* unappetizingly between *Of Mice and Men* and *The Catcher in the Rye*. Laughter had given way to diligence, three-to-five-page essays, and much class discussion about the individual and the community. I do not remember the text this time as much as the small print and the pulpy paper. I had oral surgery the week we "did" Jane Austen, and I read the book while lying on my pink bed, in my pink-carpeted bedroom, with tea bags packed into my mouth to stop the bleeding. Sliding mirror doors on my closet reflected a swollen-mouthed and melancholy fifteen-year-old. I stood out among the Polynesian and Asian kids at school because of my extremely fair skin. "Why are you so white?" everyone asked me; if my classmates were in a mood to tease, they called me "shark bait." I tried to imagine myself among the fair-skinned girls in *Pride and Prejudice*, but such escapism cut into my self-pity, so I didn't allow myself to enter Austen's world for long. Surely, I thought, Elizabeth's younger sisters would have dismissed me as a "freckled little thing."

I did not open *Pride and Prejudice* again until I was in college. I had exchanged the tropical island of my childhood for the bricks and snow of Cambridge, where I was an English and philosophy concentrator at Harvard. I had many friends in college, and to my great joy, my complexion was no longer a topic of conversation. My first story had been accepted for publication; I had earned advanced standing and placed into a sophomore English tutorial. All this had restored my self-confidence. Once again a precocious initiate into the mysteries of English literature, I now looked at Jane Austen from a critical perspective. My tutor was a Henry James specialist, and my father had given me a volume of the novelist's book reviews, in which, always incisive but rarely generous, James turned a jaundiced eye on his literary predecessors. It was in college, with James on my reading list and my own professional aspirations in mind, that I began to consider the strengths and weaknesses of *Pride and Prejudice*—the liveliness of Lizzie and her sisters, against the inarticulate stiffness of Darcy.

Granted, Darcy is supposed to be proud and rigid, silent in his dignity, but on this reading I faulted Austen for failing to provide a better view of his mind and heart. I felt she spent more time describing the contents of Darcy's house than developing his character. Darcy is shown early as a figure of unapproachable hauteur and later as a Prince Charming. His motives and interests are objects of intense speculation, but he himself remains a cipher. I began to think him a weak point in the novel, to feel that, as James says of Daniel Deronda, "He is not a man at all," but a construct. Even at the end of the book, when his transformation is complete, Darcy cannot, or, more accurately, is not allowed to, explain how he came to love Elizabeth. She insists on speaking for him, telling him exactly why he was attracted to her. "The fact is, that you were sick of civility, of deference, of officious attention. You were disgusted with the women who were always speaking and looking, and thinking for *your* approbation alone. I roused, and interested you, because I was so unlike *them*." Elizabeth's bossy, authorial little speech only calls attention to the shameless fairy-tale ending Austen has set up. The novel originally titled "First Impressions" leaves the reader with a final impression that the noble, handsome, fabulously wealthy Darcy is indeed a figment of his author's lively, feminine imagination. He has moved from grudging to admiring appreciation of Elizabeth's performances. But he is always quiet—a passive character, if an excellent audience.

My professors taught me to consider the cultural context of literary works, the social mores delineated, and the position of the author in her world. The more I learned about Jane Austen's England, the more I understood how unrealistic Darcy's second proposal is. The more I learned of Austen's own life, the more I understood how improbable Elizabeth's conquest would have been. At nine, I'd loved *Pride and Prejudice* for its humor; at fifteen, I'd read it with melancholy; but in college, I spurned it with feelings akin to those of my roommate when she broke up with her high-school sweetheart. Henry James was so much darker, so much more worldly, so sophisticated. Austen's art seemed merely sunny. She was a watercolorist, while James was the brilliant mannerist, dazzling with his chiaroscuro. *The Portrait of a Lady* numbed me, then stung me, and finally overwhelmed me. *The Wings of the Dove* entirely turned my head. *Pride and Prejudice* slipped, along with *Huckleberry Finn*, into the pile of slim books from home that I'd enjoyed when I was younger. I glanced through it only to dismiss it, and then I left it behind—seemingly forever.

I'd written books and more stories of my own, drafted my dissertation on Samuel Johnson's edition of Shakespeare, married, had two children, and moved back to Cambridge by the time I picked up *Pride and Prejudice* again. I'd just come home from my mother's funeral. I was twenty-nine and had never felt so old. My mother had died of brain cancer soon after turning fifty-one.

It was October, raining hard, and I was alone in the house with our baby. My brother-in-law was getting married that weekend, but I'd found I couldn't force myself to go to the wedding. My husband flew with our four-year-old to Philadelphia.

The rain poured down all the first night and kept coming

the next day. It was too wet to take the baby out, so he played on the floor and I listened to the rain. It rattled on the skylight in the stairwell and thrummed the roof, and I began to reread *Pride and Prejudice*. I read the book slowly and uncritically, lying on our new blue sofa in our new sparsely furnished town house. I read it because my mother had loved Jane Austen and because rereading it for solace was something she might have done. I read it because my mother was like Jane Austen in her wit, her love of irony, and her concision. My mother was shrewd like Austen, and ingenious; she flourished in difficult professional situations. And like Austen, my mother had died young with her work unfinished.

It rained all day, and I kept reading steadily. I didn't laugh, but I smiled at Mr. Bennet and Mr. Collins and Lady Catherine de Bourgh. Mr. Darcy didn't bother me at all, but strode into the book, a dashing hero brooking no doubt or literary disappointment. Perhaps he was only a figure of romance, and perhaps Pemberley was just Austen's castle in the air. The romance and the castle were no less powerful for their escapist construction. Indeed, what I found irresistible this time was the way Austen combines astute social satire with fairy tale. The combination did not seem awkward to me, but inspired. The satire is exquisite, while the fairy tale is viscerally satisfying. How delightful to watch Elizabeth rise like Cinderella above the impediments of her mother and her younger sisters! Her mother is not wicked, but she is thoughtless and vulgar. Her sisters, with the exception of Jane, are pedantic, insipid, and lusty, and, as such, throw as many obstacles in Elizabeth's way as if sabotage had been their intent. And, of course, Mr. Bingley's sisters supply their own venom. Naturally, the obstacles make Elizabeth's victory more delicious. Hers is the triumph of wit over vulgarity, self-respect over sycophancy. Until this reading, I had never appreciated Austen's fairy tale so well, but perhaps I had never needed it so much. No one dies in *Pride and Prejudice*—not even of embarrassment, as feckless Lydia and Wickham demonstrate. I no longer faulted the book for its cheerfulness or made invidious comparisons with Henry James. A dark imagination is, perhaps, more appealing before you know anything about darkness.

It is the joining of satire and fairy tale that continues to draw me to *Pride and Prejudice*, and I have been thinking about this aspect recently, after my fifth reading. This time, Elizabeth's tour of Pemberley with her aunt and uncle drew me particularly. I wondered at Austen's extensive discussion of the house—"a large, handsome, stone building, standing well on rising ground, and backed by a ridge of high woody hills"—and grounds, which are described both from the perspective of the visitors driving into the estate and through Elizabeth's eyes as she looks out a window at "the hill, crowned with wood, from which they had descended."

Austen does not generally layer on description. Her chapters are airy, uncluttered rooms, not the heavily draped, fringed, and flocked apartments of Dickens. Thus, the detail she devotes to Darcy's estate is striking. Certainly, Austen is providing a catalog of all the riches Elizabeth has refused.

She allows Elizabeth to contemplate the beauties of Pemberley with a poignant mixture of admiration, defensive pride, and regret. As Elizabeth and the Gardiners visit and then revisit Pemberley at Darcy's invitation, Austen reports on the stream stocked with fish, the fine woods, and even the splendid food served: "cold meat, cake, and a variety of all the finest fruits in season." All these demonstrate Darcy's wealth, and also his graciousness, as he extends an invitation to Mr. Gardiner to come fishing, takes the ladies walking, and insists on bringing Elizabeth to meet his sister. Before, these scenes at Pemberley had seemed to me unduly fanciful. I'd felt the action slow, and grown tired of the contrivances by which Austen brings Elizabeth back to Darcy. On this reading, however, they seemed to me the most interesting in the novel, for here Austen truly defines the union between Elizabeth and Darcy, joining liveliness and formality, the bourgeois and the aristocratic, new forms and old in a utopian reworking of the world.

As I read the description of Pemberley, I saw Austen adopting the grand literary tradition of the country-house poem to describe Darcy's noble countryseat. Through Elizabeth's admiring eyes, Pemberley is nothing less than a Penshurst in its natural beauty, order, and elegance. Ben Jonson had praised Penshurst as a house not "built to envious show," and Pemberley succeeds as well in surpassing lesser, and newer, estates like Lady Catherine's Rosings, which are merely ostentatious and fashionable, filled with "uselessly fine" furniture. Pemberley has every virtue that Jonson listed as essential for the great country house: the grounds, the woods, the fish, the fruit in season, the bounty of nature tamed into proportion and elegance.

I had read "To Penshurst" in college, and again in graduate school, but I'd never made the connection between the poem and Austen's book. As a student of the novel, I had always looked forward. I'd studied the "rise" of the novel, the development and growth and refinement of the genre. My forward thinking was also the product of my own impatience and ambition as a writer—my eagerness to dart onto the literary stage. As a reader, I've looked forward so much that I've been surprised recently by how pleasurable it can be to look back again to earlier forms, and, as Austen might have said, to rediscover the elegant and pleasing landscapes to be found there.

Like Penshurst, Pemberley is staffed with grateful servants and surrounded by respectful townspeople. It is both a productive estate and a symbol of order for the larger society. The only thing Pemberley lacks is a mistress, and in Elizabeth, Austen provides one. Elizabeth moves Darcy to show that he can be not merely great but gracious and good. This joining of greatness and goodness defines true nobility for Austen, just as it did for Jonson. And yet she goes much further than Jonson, for in her novelistic version of the country-house poem, it is not only the lord who can say he dwells there, but the middle-class admirer who will succeed in dwelling there as well. Elizabeth, the cataloger of Pemberley's beauties— and, by extension, Austen, Elizabeth's author—takes possession of them. Elizabeth, who grows to appreciate Darcy's virtues—and, by extension, the reader, Elizabeth's confidant—comes to marry him. Ah, the wish fulfillment here is wonderful indeed, once you begin unfolding the wish in earnest.

I think unfolding is what rereading is about. Like pleated fabric, the text reveals different parts of its pattern at different times. And yet every time the text unfolds, in the library, or in bed, or upon the grass, the reader adds new wrinkles. Memory and experience press themselves into each reading so that each encounter informs the next.

Is it possible that if you read *Pride and Prejudice* too young, the book is ruined for you? At what age should you read Jane Austen? At fifteen? Or twenty-nine? At thirty-six? Austen wrote the novel when she was just twenty. It would be strange for the reader to wait until she was older than the author. Can children grow into or out of books, as they grow into and out of clothes? I reread the novel because I read it at nine. I return to it not because it is the best novel I have read, or the most important, but because of the memories and wishes I've folded in its pages—because on every reading I see old things in it.

Lawrence by Lightning

The Virgin and the Gypsy, by D. H. Lawrence

rowing up within the tightly guarded confines of a fifteenth-century English boarding school, my friends and I took as our tokens of accomplishment the somewhat recherché gray volumes known as Penguin Modern Classics. When I was in college, in the mid-1970s, Picador books would become the rage (Hunter Thompson, Tom Wolfe, Richard Brautigan—outlaw American energy packaged as real literature!); and, a decade later, in the sleek Manhattan of the 1980s, the Vintage Contemporaries series (born, it seemed, out of *Bright Lights, Big City*) would have a special cachet as some of us hobbled off to Area at 3:00 a.m. But in 1972, in rural, changeless England, where our allowances were scarcely large enough to stretch to three packages of McVitie's digestives every six months, and where we had to attend chapel twice a day, Latin hymns on Sunday nights, and class at 7:30 a.m.—all in white tie and tails—we could think of no better way to distinguish ourselves than through amassing these formidable gray paperbacks on our shelves.

Canetti, Čapek, Svevo, Vian: even now the names, nearly all foreign and unpronounceable, reek of forbidden cigarettes and the cafés we weren't allowed to visit. To this day I remember next to nothing of these books, and even the authors' names are increasingly strange to me. But in anxious adolescence, they were the last word, so it seemed, in worldliness and sophistication, to be displayed beside our beds like the conquests (in this all-male internment camp) we hadn't made. The funeral-black Penguin Classics—Xenophon and Sir Thomas More and Plutarch—were too much like everything we were trying to escape; the jaunty contemporary orange Penguins—Laurie Lee and Keith Waterhouse and Kingsley Amis—seemed too much a part of the dreary English landscape all around; but the Penguin Modern Classics—*The Magic Mountain*, *The Counterfeiters*, *Nausea*—were everything we sought (and found most efficiently, as it happened, in the cinema, among Pasolini renditions of Boccaccio and Chaucer)—namely, grown-up European works of high culture that packed the punch of illicit magazines.

Occasionally, almost flukily, a volume would surface that had so much to do with adolescent boys escaping from their military surroundings (and brandishing, as status symbols, philosophical tomes) that we would actually read it in its entirety and with a palpitating, almost awestruck sense of recognition. Alain-Fournier's *Le grand Meaulnes* was one such work, inevitably, with its haunting evocation of a paradise glimpsed in boyhood and never found again; Raymond

Radiguet's *Le diable au corps* (or *The Devil in the Flesh*, as it was translated for us) was another, a highly French tale of an eighteen-year-old boy taking on an older mistress, which convinced us all we were actually Frenchmen under the skin. A fifteen-year-old housemate (now, of course, one of England's most distinguished moral voices) once slipped me a copy of Hesse's *Narziss and Goldmund* with the blunt Anglo-Saxon commendation, "It's got a hundred screws."

I read it immediately, and almost instantly felt at home in it: not only because of its austere gray cover, depicting a chestnut tree outside a wintry monastery that looked uncannily similar to the monastery-in-mufti where we were working on our chastity, poverty, and obedience; and not only because of its earnest, almost sacramental hallowing of a friendship between two young men, one immersed in the world of books, the other committed to finding the meaning of life through a series of adventures (in short, as my friend had promised, an archetypal Hellenic quest with R-rated props); but also, I suppose, because—like all our favorite books—it was about a seeker pledged to the holiness of the heart's affections and committed to individuality at any cost. (Much later, I would see that part of its appeal might even have had to do with the fact that it was the only common link between my surplice-choired medieval school and the vagrant hippie California of my parents' home, to which I returned on holidays—and, of course, it took that very commute, the dialogue between Apollo and Dionysus, as its theme.)

But before I could fall completely under Hesse's spell, another book came along that touched a sudden flame in me in some more mysterious way. D. H. Lawrence's novella *The Virgin and the Gypsy* (written not long before his death, in France, in 1930, and found only after it) was an orange Penguin of the kind we affected to despise, and came from someone as much of the countryside around us as the Huxleys and Orwells we were force-fed in class (and the poems that rhymed with the memorial plaques that surrounded us—"Dulce et decorum est pro patria mori"). Yet it had to it something foreign and subversive that seemed to place it among the gray books we regarded as canonical. Part of its attraction came no doubt from the photograph it bore on its cover—of the Canadian actress Joanna Shimkus, as ethereal and undefiled as a Botticelli angel, looking into the distance as she is approached by a movie Minotaur (Franco Nero, then at the height of his fame). Part of it no doubt came from its bringing together of young English girl and alien wanderer—as if Narziss and Goldmund were of different sexes, and could interact in newly electric ways! But whatever the source of its magic, as familiar and unfathomed as a loved one, I opened the book on the afternoon of my fifteenth birthday, and closed it that evening, feeling that a chapter in my boyhood now had ended.

Later, of course, I would find any number of clearer reasons for the way in which it possessed me. Virgins and gypsies were the two kinds of beings most outside our orbit then, and most subject to our fascination; and Lawrence's heroic energy, his unvarnished romanticism, his relentless, burning determination to tell a story about a young and inexperienced soul awakening to its destiny (its passion), were guar-

anteed to appeal to overeducated inmates like ourselves. The
book was everything that was denied us (girls and movement
and rebellion). It was escape—from the dark and drafty class-
rooms on whose desks 530 years of predecessors had scribbled
their names; from the unreal rites of reciting the principal
parts of the Greek verb βαίνω (I walk) in our pajamas and
then donning black robes to go to class at dawn; from, in fact,
all the cultural weight and sense of expectation embodied by
those Penguin Modern Classics.

But it was something more than that, too. At college a
few years later (where beginning students of literature were
allowed to read "modern" authors for their first year only—
"modern" meaning later than 1832, though earlier than
1945), Lawrence was far and away the most explosive novelist on offer—and, we soon found, the only male novelist,
other than Henry James, that girls seemed to like, too. And
there was something about his raw, passionate intensity,
scrupulously unrevised and incorrigibly restless, that felt (as
Emily Brontë did) like the way we might write in our diaries, if we admitted to keeping them. Not forbidding like
Joyce, not rich with metropolitan polish like Woolf, Lawrence
came across as less a text than a man, shouting in our ears.

When finally I succeeded in falling in love (in a kind of
Virgin and Gypsy episode with the characters reversed), I
found myself reading the final sentences of *Lady Chatterley's
Lover* aloud to my new companion (the book's original title,
"Tenderness," catching all the luminous sweetness and almost elegiac vulnerability of Lawrence in his final years, his
strident dogmatism giving way to something more human

and gentle, delivered in a spirit of farewell). I made my way back to his story "Love Among the Haystacks," and was so moved by its air of protective intimacy that I paid it homage in the only way I could—by concocting a similar romance, set in the university library, that I called "Love Among the A Stacks." In the same volume, I came upon Lawrence's last story, "The Man Who Died," and was so stunned by its tale of the risen Jesus, aching with incompleteness, and the priestess of Isis who ministers to his wounds that I wheedled the Oxford University Arts Society into giving me a grant to turn it into a film.

But as the years passed, and my initial excitement in discovering freedom and love subsided a little, Lawrence fell away from me a little, too. Studying English and more English, as if longing to profess it (from the age of seventeen to the age of twenty-five—it seems insane to me now—I studied nothing but English literature, with even American literature generally regarded as beyond the pale), I turned to Lawrence whenever I wanted a jolt of electricity, something visionary and intoxicating to raise me above the day-to-day world— and, better yet, to a world whose contours were lined with gold. And whenever I traveled, I read what Lawrence had written about the place I was visiting, since he caught everywhere he saw with a quick impatience that put traditional "travel writers" to shame. When I went to Australia in 1988, the only guidebook of any use was *Kangaroo*, written more than sixty years earlier after a stay of only a few weeks; in the California where I had lived for thirty years, I never found the description to better Lawrence's dashed-off assessment in a letter:

> A queer place—in a way, it has turned its back on the world, and looks into the void Pacific. It is absolutely selfish, very empty, but not false, and at least not full of false effort. . . . It's a sort of crazy sensible. Just the moment: hardly as far ahead as *carpe diem*.

I even drove across country more than once, sleeping in my car, to visit the small hut above Taos where Lawrence had lived among the pines.

Yet the feeling always lingered, especially as I learned to read with a "critical" eye, that Lawrence was one of those enthusiasms of youth that one put away with childish things, like Hesse, in fact (or their radiant disciple Henry Miller). He was never very far away from me—the pale, blazing figure in the corner whose eyes won't leave you alone—but he was so much himself, I felt, at every moment and in every sentence, that he could not easily be fit into someone else's life. (This must have been the problem for those who met him, too, and found themselves stranded between impatience and love.) Lawrence existed so far outside the usual categories—it was hard to assign him a race, a class, even at times a gender—that he could not be assimilated into any system. He had something in common with all the great English writers who railed against English narrowness and skepticism (Graham Greene and Somerset Maugham, John Berger and John le Carré), but he remained redoubtably an odd man out. And where the other unassimilable mavericks, like Melville and Thoreau, were apostles of aloneness, Lawrence insisted on bringing his ungovernable singularity to the theme of human connectedness, the sparks of divinity that fly between one soul and another.

Then, a few months ago, Lawrence unexpectedly gate-crashed my life again. An Englishman from Hollywood came to see me, interested in adapting a romance I'd written many years before, and as his calling card and letter of reference he gave me a script he'd just written, based on an early Lawrence novel. The best reader I know suddenly got in touch to tell me to read Geoff Dyer's *Out of Sheer Rage*, a portrait of Lawrence so Lawrentian that it never actually addresses its subject or gets round to discussing most of his books (being content, instead, to loose a Lawrentian fury against the very notion of biography and, of course, against the unchanging stiffness and conventionalism of England). The passages from Lawrence's letters that Dyer included in his meanderings shone like sparklers held up on a chill November evening, at a Guy Fawkes party in the Midlands, by a stranger who stands so close to you that you can see his breath condense in the dark.

That same month, an old friend from northern California called to ask whether I'd be interested in helping him work up a film based on "The Man Who Died" (the same project I'd hatched twenty years earlier)—though before I could an-swer he got caught in a tragicomic whirl over the screen

rights that ended, a few months later, with the discovery that
they belonged to a mysterious Italian fugitive whose ex-
partners said, "He is either in America—or Hell!"

It was time, clearly, to put aside all these imperfect reflections of Lawrence and read the man himself again. I was
now almost exactly the same age he had been when he embarked upon his great final period (lit up, as Keats's last
months were, by a flicker of almost posthumous radiance
that sometimes seems to accompany the final stages of tuberculosis). More than that, I'd reached the point in life in
which I was not so often discovering new writers as constantly rediscovering old ones, going back again and again to
Love's Labour's Lost and *Of Human Bondage*, and to the letters of Keats in which he says that a "World of Pains" is necessary to "school an Intelligence and make it a soul." Besides,
I was now a world away from England and adolescence, living in a small apartment in the Japanese countryside where
not freedom but seclusion seemed the greatest luxury.

One dark December afternoon, while the sweet-potato
salesman outside played his unbearably melancholy traditional song and a child across the way picked out a simple
melody on his piano, I dug up a copy of the tale that had so
consumed me once, and returned to the damp English north.
Almost instantly, of course, I found that nothing was as I remembered it: the virgin and the gypsy scarcely meet in all the
brief eighty-five pages—everything is intimation and fleet-
ing glances—and their bond is not even explicitly consum-
mated. The teenage boy in search of forbidden excitements
could have been only partially delighted by "The absolutely

naked insinuation of desire made her lie prone and powerless in the bed as if a drug had cast her in a new, molten
mould."

I could see now, in fact, that the story had as much to do
with class as with sex, and really was nothing more than a
cry for release from the stifling puritanism and hypocrisies
of English provincial life (a life I'd never known). Two
young girls—Yvette, the virgin of the title, and her sister,
Lucille—return from a "finishing year" in Lausanne, all fur
collars and chic hats, to the ugly stone house of their father's
rectory, where he, one Arthur Saywell, sits like a frightened
frog, wrestling for power with his mother, his sister, and a
brother in "an atmosphere of cunning self-sanctification."
The girls' glamorous mother, "She-who-was-Cynthia," who
stands for everything quick and flowing in them, is never in
evidence (she having long since run away from this Horlicks
Hell); and every time one of the young women opens a window in search of "fresh air," Granny slams it shut, com-
plaining of the "draughts."

As all that suggests, *The Virgin and the Gypsy* is written
with the kind of naked self-forgetfulness that Lawrence
made his own. There is little subtlety or surprise in it, and
you know, really, as soon as you see the title (even without
Joanna Shimkus on the cover), what will happen, and what it
all means. Uncle Fred is a "stingy and grey-faced man of
forty, who just lived dingily for himself"; Aunt Cissie is "pale,
pious and gnawed by an inward worm"; even the back-cover
blurb talks routinely of "the stifling confines of home and
family" and the "elemental force" that "threatens the con-

ventional fabric of Yvette's existence." And that force is embodied, far too conveniently, by a married itinerant laborer "with full, conceited, impudent black eyes," whom Yvette meets when her family car almost collides with his gypsy cart.

Yet what is more startling, perhaps, especially to one long past adolescence, is how this most familiar and predictable of stories—scarcely more than a Harlequin romance, it seems, of a pale girl rescued by a dark manly creature of the wild— is made something more, simply through the intensity and conviction Lawrence pours into it. On a sentence-by-sentence level, it is almost irredeemably sloppy and banal ("Feelings are so complicated" is about as subtle as the synopsis of Yvette's inner life gets); yet burning through the sentences, and flickering at their corners, is a fire that cannot be easily ignored.

You read Lawrence, I came to see, almost entirely by flashes of lightning. Whole stretches are flat and quite unremarkable; it's almost better not to take in the descriptions of "the mysterious fruit of her virginity" or "the rather resentful brown eyes of a spoilt Jewess"; the virtually unintelligible digression about how the "widow of a knighted doctor, a harmless person indeed, had become an obnoxity in their lives" (a what?); or Yvette's recognition that the gypsy looked at her as if "he really, but *really*, *desired* me." And yet, almost by the same token, the whole thing shines, often, with a white-hot intensity that (as in Emily Brontë again) has the power to pick you up and transport you like the wind rattling against the windowpanes. I found myself reading the story as quickly as Lawrence had no doubt written it, and so reading it (as, again, I'm sure it was written) not so much with the conscious mind as with the senses and the instincts.

In a certain respect, in fact, Lawrence's prose enacts the very liberation it describes, speaking to one as the gypsy does, and touching something unprotected and soft, something virginal, that makes one feel as if cynicism is a distant country. There are no half measures here (every sentence is thrown down like a dare, even as it contradicts one in the previous paragraph), and Lawrence writes as if under the possession of a spirit that does not allow him to linger over details or niceties.

It is this, perhaps, that helps him get us to care for Yvette as wholly and solicitously as he clearly does. She is an archetypal heroine from his later period—all tenderness and longing, a moist snow flower waiting for her spring. But she is also a typical nineteen-year-old—flighty, proud, selfish, and spoiled (her "soft, virgin, heedless candor," as he writes, is responsible for "her admirers and her enemies"). Yvette, he tells us, with a saving detachment, "was born inside the pale. And she loved comfort, and a certain prestige." Even her wish to "fall *violently* in love" is, in a certain light, absurd (she "seemed always to imagine," he writes, "that someone would come along singing *Tirra-lirra!* or something equally intelligent, by the river").

Yet in the midst of all this, there is something else in her, something indefinable—a flame, or candle, inside her being—

that Lawrence tends to zealously. To a remarkable extent, he sits inside her being—one reason why one of the great androgynous writers has always appealed to women as much as to men—and cheers her spirit on. "There is something about me which they don't see and never would see," she thinks at one point, and Lawrence acts as the custodian of that hidden angel, bringing it forth with all the understanding of a spirit no less intuitive and rebellious and turned toward heaven.

Of course, I thought, in my elder self, an adolescent boy in a boarding school would thrill to this tale of a spirit inside him that no one but he can recognize (the theme of Hesse, again, and of all our favorite questers). And Lawrence, writing with a furious, headlong, hit-or-miss abandon, catches some of these sensations as one would a flame. (I recalled that part of his force came from the fact that he revised not by tinkering with words or polishing cadences but by writing the whole manuscript—all five hundred pages of it, if need be—out from scratch again, so as to catch that heedless momentum.) But I also saw that a teenage boy would have been stirred less by the heroine's "bare upper arms"—or by the fact that she, like him, is longing for real experience (with, as Lawrence insists, someone other than a boarding-school boy)—than by lines like "On her face was that tender look of sleep, which a nodding flower has when it is full out."

At the climax of the brief story, both these strands—the absolute looseness of the brute judgments and repetitions, and the light shining within and in spite of them—come together dramatically. Suddenly, after a flash flood in a nearby river, the waters rise outside the rectory and begin to pour into the garden, where Yvette is sitting on a nostalgic spring afternoon (the former graduate student in me rolling his eyes at the heavy-handedness of the symbolism). "She was barely conscious: as if the flood was in her soul," Lawrence writes, in defiance of every ascetic precept taught in literature classes. At that very moment, of course, the gypsy shows up, pulls her out to safety, and, while hated Granny dies, is obliged to strip off his clothes and take the naked Yvette into his arms to protect her from the rising wind and waters.

Yet just as everything seems to be dwindling into caricature, Lawrence defers, as few writers do, to mystery. The dark animal wanderer holds the virgin princess in his arms— the moment we've been waiting for all along—and that is all he seems to do. At precisely the instant when we most expect Lawrence to fulminate, he rises into silence (as he does earlier in the story when Yvette visits a fortune-teller and, miraculously, follows her into a caravan so we never learn what passes between them). There is a numinousness at the heart of the tale (and of his conception of the link between his characters) that Lawrence has the sense not to mess with, and as the story drifts into the fragile, intimate moments of his later period, its mysterious beauty is of the same kind you feel when the priestess washes Jesus' wounds in "The Man Who Died," or the woman who gets on a horse in Mexico simply rides away into the mountains. Geoffrey meets the sodden Lydia in the haystacks and just shelters her all night, in a communion more moving than any love scene I can think of; the gypsy sends Yvette a letter on the final page—

Lady Chatterley again—and we learn for the first time that he has a name.

I thought back, closing the book in my modern Japanese apartment, to the fifteen-year-old in his little cell, devouring the whole story in an afternoon, and I saw that something more valuable than his prurience, or even his nascent sense of romanticism, was being encouraged. Escape was less the point than a kind of tenderness that could flicker into something higher. And I thought even more of the fledgling student of literature embarking on a ten-year course of learning to read books by breaking them down into pieces. Like almost no other writer I can think of, with the exception of Melville or the Shakespeare of Poor Tom (or such idiosyncratic forces as Arundhati Roy or Keri Hulme), Lawrence refuses to let you read him in that way: either you surrender to him, and to a spirit that flings out every sentence as if it were its last, or you are condemned to remain forever on the sidelines.

As someone trying to be a writer now myself, and thus more concerned than ever with carefulness and craft, with all the prohibitions that watchfulness creates, I think I heard Lawrence even more powerfully than I had twenty-five years before, enjoining me to read and listen with the soul (as he does, preeminently, in his *Studies in Classic American Literature*), and taking me precisely to those areas where words are of no use. Lawrence approaches the world, his characters, and even the reader as if he were their lover (and an impatient, restless lover at that), and taking him on his own terms, as one has to do, I hardly had the consciousness to notice that the story—now in its twenty-eighth printing—comes these days with a cover image of a young woman staring into a fire bright as lightning (the movie version having long since been forgotten). Its elegant gray spine proclaims it to be now, as it had not been in 1972, a Penguin Modern Classic.

The Ice Palace

"The Snow Queen," by Hans Christian Andersen

hree a.m., bolt awake. It's late November above the Arctic Circle. The body insists it's time to get up, even though it won't be light until—when?—nine-thirty, and only a pale blue light then. I crossed nine time zones to arrive in Stockholm, traveled seventeen hours north by train to Kiruna. I've come to spend the winter in Arctic Scandinavia, first stop the old Sami village of Jukkasjärvi by the frozen Torne River, where every year a team of builders, artists, and amateurs comes together to reshape what melted in the spring: a hotel made of mounded snow and blocks and columns of blue river ice.

My cabin is warm. Outside, snow falls. Most of the possessions I'll have with me for the next three months—laptop, journal, long underwear, woolens, calcium pills with extra vitamin D—lie strewn about. I'm never tidy when I travel; I need to take over my temporary spaces completely. I make a cup of coffee, take out a folder of photocopied pages and a library book.

I'm going to reread "The Snow Queen" the way I always dreamed I'd read it, not in the twee Danish town of Odense, which has made an industry of Hans Christian Andersen, but up here in the North, in the wintery land of reindeer. As a child in Southern California, I dreamed of snowy landscapes but never saw a single flake. Every December my friends and I heard familiar songs: "I'm Dreaming of a White Christmas," "Frosty the Snowman," and "Jingle Bells." As the sun beat down, some of our neighbors turned their yards into Santa's Workshop or sprayed white stuff on their trees. Illustrated books showed cottages half-buried in white, snowmen out front, with children in caps and jackets throwing snowballs. We knew the forts and figures were made of snow, but what *was* snow? Was it very cold, like ice cream, or was it more like the spangled white felt that surrounded the base of the Christmas tree in our living room? The only snowflakes we knew were the ones we cut, painstakingly, from folded white paper in school. Was snow frozen rain? No, it must be soft, we thought, a silent satin coverlet.

What about ice? Ice cubes we knew, snow cones and Popsicles. But up in Alaska and the North Pole there were houses of ice—the igloos of the Eskimos, the palace of the Snow Queen. That far north, Christmas wasn't just white, it was perpetual. I'd never even owned a coat. What would the cold feel like? Sleeping in an igloo must be like climbing into the freezer at the ice cream shop and having the lid close over you.

I pull out one of the photocopied versions of "The Snow Queen," taken from *The Pink Fairy Book*. *The Pink Fairy Book*, along with the *Green*, *Lilac*, *Yellow*, and so on, was edited by Andrew Lang and first published in the late nineteenth century. I read the library editions as a child. We had few books in our house beyond the Bible and the complete works of Mary Baker Eddy. Nevertheless, we were avid librarygoers, my mother and I, and when I wasn't reading *Christian Science Sentinel* stories for children, I was reading fairy tales. The Lang books were my passport to Grimm, Perrault, and Andersen; I checked them out over and over. I believe my mother thought they were as innocent and uplifting as the tales about children praying, not precisely to be healed, but to keep their thinking clear and right.

It's utterly silent and utterly black except for the pool of light outside my window, which illuminates a deep drift of snow and snowflakes—"white bees," Andersen calls them—buzzing by. I slip into the story of Kai and Gerda, a tale of friendship frozen into ice and redeemed by faithful love, as if placing on an old turntable an LP I've heard a thousand times. The pictures are as I remember them, bold but languid, vaguely Pre-Raphaelite. The women wear swirling cloaks and clingy, high-waisted skirts that show the outlines of their strong, elongated thighs. "The Snow Queen Appears

to Kai" seems to bear more than a passing resemblance to
Botticelli's *Venus*.

I read about the troll who invents a mirror "which had
the strange power of being able to make anything good or
beautiful that it reflected appear horrid; and all that was evil
and worthless seem attractive and worthwhile." When the
troll takes the mirror up to heaven to make fun of God and
the angels, he loses his grip on it, and it falls and breaks into
billions of pieces, some of which are turned into windowpanes or spectacles, and many of which become tiny glass
splinters that get into people's eyes and make them see
things askew and cruelly. I read about the splinters that
lodge in Kai's eye and his heart; about his semi-willing ab-
duction by the Snow Queen; about his friend Gerda's long
journey to find him and love him back to himself. I read
slowly, but it's over too soon.

It was twelve years ago that I first reread "The Snow
Queen." The story had been important to me as a child, and
I went back to Andersen's tale as I began to pull together
fragments of memories and past influences for a memoir
about my Christian Science childhood. At the time I was
struggling to make sense of a religion that had instilled such
trust in God's love—and in the certainty that all was for the
best in this best of all possible worlds—that it had left me
completely unprepared for a string of family disasters. The
memoir tells the story of my mother's crisis of faith when
she discovered she had breast cancer; of her breakdown and
the suicide attempt that left her disfigured; of her suffering
and death and my losses as a child. The metaphor of the

splintered mirror offered a means of exploring how people who said they loved you (your parents, for example) could change into unrecognizable beings who would abandon you for the icy necessity of death or for another woman (my father's second wife, a classic wicked stepmother). It was with Kai that I identified on that reading. I felt as if I too had long had an icy splinter inside me, a splinter that had gradually frozen my heart.

But now, reading "The Snow Queen" in Lapland, I see how much of the tale is taken up by Gerda's great adventure, out into, as Andersen calls it several times, "the wide world." When she loses her dearest childhood friend—first psychologically, through the splinters that turn him sour and cynical, and then, in reality, to the powerful and seductive Snow Queen—Gerda sets off on an epic journey to find him. Never wavering in her belief that he is alive, she sails, walks, rides in a carriage, and is carried by a reindeer to the Snow Queen's palace, where Kai has been doing little but racking his brain over broken pieces of ice, trying to spell a forgotten word.

Yesterday I crunched and squeaked my way through the halls and suites of the Ice Hotel, taking photographs and talking with an architect who told me he'd modeled his design of the vault like corridors on Antonio Gaudí's strange cathedral masterpiece, La Sagrada Família. The mounds of snow, bulldozed onto steel forms, had become disorienting tunnels with white floors, ceilings, and walls. Opaque and soft-looking, the snow nevertheless was hard to the touch, the crystals packed into weight-bearing walls. All sound was muffled; it was impossible to hear voices in the next room because snow acts as a sound barrier. I had the impression both of being buried alive and of being in a sacred space, a Cistercian monastery or a Greek Orthodox chapel. The white solidity of the snow was balanced by the transparency of the pillars and blocks of ice. During the day the ice was a radiant blue, the light broken and refracted hundreds of times by joints and crackings. Light is captured and magnified by ice; even under the workers' artificial floodlights, the ice took on unearthly sheens and glitters.

Well wrapped in my insulated clothes and red hat and mittens, I stomped my feet and breathed clouds of mist in suites where chain saws roared and chisels chinked, where artists attacked massive blocks of ice, creating everything from tables and chairs to beds to statues and friezes. Some of the designs were free-spirited (the Rock 'n' Roll Room, with its homage to the Fender guitar) or kitschy (the Viking Room, with its bed in the shape of a dragon-headed ship— "Especially popular with Americans," I was told). Other suites were designed by minimalists, with bulging snow beds and undulant columns of ice. In an ecstasy of cold, I wandered around for hours before dipping back into the warmth of my cabin to write up notes.

"It's really not so cold to sleep in the Ice Hotel," everyone told me. "Snow is an insulator. It only gets down to five in here, even though it might be twenty or thirty outside." No one ever says "minus" here during the winter; it's just assumed. I'm planning to come back in a couple of months, when the hotel is finished, to take a room overnight. Somehow I'm not convinced that sleeping on a bed of ice, even on a layer of reindeer skins, even inside a thermal sleeping bag, will be especially cozy. (Fast-forward: It's not. Though it is strange and beautiful.)

In my memory, the Snow Queen's palace absorbed most of the narrative. Its descriptions acted on me like an icy aphrodisiac:

> The castle walls were of the driven snow, and the windows and doors of the biting winds. There were more than a hundred halls, according to the way the snow drifted; the biggest stretched for many miles, all lit up by the intense Northern Lights; and they were so big, so bare, so icy cold, and so sparkling.

I am surprised now to find that so little of the fairy tale takes place in the palace. In fact, there are almost as many descriptions of sunshine and flowers as of snow. Did I forget them because these things were so normal to a California child? Andersen, who often traveled to Italy and claimed he felt more himself in warm and sensuous climes, lavishes description on the little window boxes between Gerda's and Kai's attic apartments, and on the cherry orchard and garden of the wise old woman who takes Gerda in. The book ends with a vision of a garden too—Eden restored after the cold trials of the North.

Andersen's descriptions of ice owe much to his imagination. Now that I'm actually up above the Arctic Circle with my maps and guidebooks, I'm aware of just how vague

Andersen's geography and meteorology are. He puts Lapland near the North Pole, and makes the snow and ice perpetual. In reality, Lapland is far enough south to experience all four seasons; it's not Italy, but some summer days can be positively balmy. Even the Ice Hotel melts in late April.

I make a second cup of coffee and take out a copy of another translation, this one by Erik Christian Haugaard, a bilingual Danish author who put together *Hans Christian Andersen: The Complete Fairy Tales and Stories* twenty-seven years ago. This is the version I read when I was working on my memoir. I'm shocked at how lively the writing is, at how much more *story* there is than in the *Pink Fairy Book* tale, which is, I now notice for the first time, "Translated from the German of Hans Andersen by Miss Alma Alleyne." I compare the two. Miss Alma Alleyne's condensed and bowdlerized translation has left out whole sections, such as Gerda's encounters with the wise old woman's flowers, each of whom tells a different story. Again I read slowly; again I think, This is really about Gerda, out in the wide world, discovering herself.

It's still only 6:00 a.m. I rummage through my things, find a Luna bar and an apple, and eat them. Now I open a collection of Andersen's tales in Danish that I picked up yesterday at the Kiruna library. (During my three months of travel in Scandinavia, I'll often be allowed to check out books overnight by trusting librarians.) I've never read Andersen before in his original language, but Danish isn't difficult if you know Norwegian. People often assume that because I translate Norwegian, I must be Norwegian myself. In fact, I had a grandmother who emigrated from Sweden as a child with her family, as well as a grandfather who came from the southwest of Ireland, arriving alone in Boston at fourteen. My Stockholm-born grandmother died in childbirth; my father was sent to an orphanage, and then adopted. Later, when he found his grandparents again, he discovered they spoke Swedish, or English with heavy accents. Their language died with them. My father never thought to learn it, preferring Latin instead.

I know Norwegian because of a few summer jobs, and then because its literature began to interest me enormously. In days gone by, when there was more time, educated people often learned a language, or several, in order to read important authors. I suppose that's how I've felt about Norwegian. Relatively few literary works in Norwegian have crossed into English; when I read fiction and poetry in the original, new worlds opened up. I also found how rich the experience of reading another language could be when I succumbed to a different rhythm and tasted the flavors and shapes of unfamiliar words.

I turn to "Snedronningen," Danish for "The Snow Queen," where Andersen's quirky, confident voice immediately rings out: "Se så. Nu begynder vi." ("Well, now. Let's begin," is how I would translate it.) Andersen was famously underserved by English translators in the past (and even more recently—the opening of the Haugaard version is decidedly clunky: "All right. We will start the story"). Yet there's a colloquial dash that comes across even in Miss Alma Alleyne's translation, a sense of real speech, racy and humorous. With pleasure, I now read the original Danish through to the end, noting the places where the text can't be rendered in English with the same meaning. For instance, Gerda calls Kai her "lille legebroder," her little play-brother, which is always translated as "playmate," a tarnished English word if ever there was one.

What catches my attention on this rereading, now that I'm up in the North? Shoes and socks! What does it mean that Gerda is so often shoeless in the story? Her first act, on setting off to find Kai, is to offer her red shoes to the river. Later on she's given boots by a princess, but these are forgotten in haste. By the time she approaches the icy door of the snow palace, she's barefoot again and has to pick her way across a frozen expanse toward Kai.

Andersen was a cobbler's son, and shoes played a recurring role in his work. Another memorable Andersen tale is "The Girl Who Trod on a Loaf," a creepy story in which a selfish girl who doesn't want to get her new shoes wet puts a loaf of bread down on a puddle, and promptly sinks into a boggy purgatory in which all the flies whose wings she's torn off for sport crawl over her face. In "The Red Shoes," a poor orphan named Karen is taken in by a nearsighted old lady who, when she buys the child a pair of shoes, can't tell that they're red, not black. There's a scandal when Karen wears them to church, and the red shoes take on a life of their own, dancing away with Karen until she becomes so worn and thin that she asks an executioner to chop off her feet with his ax. (As a child growing up to believe that illness, pain, and selfish behavior were just "errors" that could be rectified by a half hour with *Science and Health*, I was shocked and thrilled at the bizarre punishments Andersen meted out to his heroines.) Gerda often has *no* shoes, and that suggests that her journey is a religious pilgrimage, with echoes of barefoot martyrdom endured for love, as well as an act of great courage and fortitude.

Reading "The Snow Queen" as Gerda's story makes me more aware of its wide array of female characters, including animals and talking flowers. Not just one, but *four* wise old women play roles in the tale. One is the grandmother at home (Kai and Gerda are said to have parents, but we never meet them, and it's never clear whose grandmother she is). Second is the old gardener who snags Gerda off the river with her shepherd's crook and uses mild magic to keep her in the cherry orchard long past summer. Later in the story, we meet first a Lapp woman, who writes a note to her friend the Finn woman on a piece of dried cod, and then the Finn woman herself, who seems to live in her sauna and who boils the cod letter in a stew pot after reading it. All these women are good witches, mild fertility figures dispensing wisdom and directions.

The Snow Queen herself is a goddess archetype of a different mold, a seductive vamp, even a polar vampire, who invites Kai to creep inside her bearskin coat:

> "Are you still cold?" she asked, and kissed his forehead. Her
> kiss was colder than ice. It went right to his heart, which was
> already half made of ice. He felt as though he were about to
> die, but it hurt only for a minute, then it was over.

She refrains from more kissing only because she knows
she'd kiss the life out of him. Seductresses are common in
nineteenth-century fiction; more intriguing to me, I find on
this rereading, is the little robber girl, who participates in the
casual killing of the coachman and servants accompanying
Gerda, and then claims Gerda for herself. "She must give me
her muff, her beautiful dress and sleep with me in my bed,"
she announces. A modern reader might well find an erotic
subtext in their night together, especially after reading Jackie
Wullschlager's recent biography, which finds ample evidence that Andersen, if not an open homosexual, definitely
had queer predilections. Butch or not, the little robber girl is
a bold and brilliant creation, as refreshingly unfeminine and
amoral as Astrid Lindgren's Pippi Longstocking (Lindgren
also wrote a novel about a robber family, *Ronia, the Robber's
Daughter*).

Yet of all the story's characters, it's Gerda who impresses
me most now. (As a child, I liked the talking reindeer best; a
dozen years ago, it was Kai who called to me; in twenty years,
perhaps I'll be most drawn to the Finn woman in her sauna.)
Gerda is steadfast, she's warmhearted, she listens to animals
and takes their advice, she's shaken but unbowed by setbacks.
Even though her feet are freezing, she enters the palace of
the Snow Queen, walks over to Kai, and sets him straight.

She has no pride; her tears fall on his breast and melt the splinters in his heart. Then *he* cries, and the splinter washes right out of his eye. And isn't that what we all want deep down? To drop the cynicism and defensiveness, to give up the mathematics of hatred, to melt the hardness of another's heart and in the process melt our own walls too?

Not all of Andersen's tales appeal to me anymore, and many make me shudder. I believe Gerda is the reason I can still reread "The Snow Queen" without gagging on the saccharine Christian symbolism that spoils some of his other works. Though there's a bit of the sentimental in the ending of the story when Gerda and Kai return by foot (Gerda presumably still without shoes) to the garden of their childhood, the effect is deeply satisfying. If our hearts are open, we *can* return to the Edens of our youth, even if we are, like Gerda and Kai, now fully grown.

Seven-thirty and still pitch-dark, but now breakfast is available in the inn across the street from the Ice Hotel. I'm starving. I put on long underwear, an Icelandic sweater, and a heavy parka. It's been in the twenties here (that's *minus* twenties), but somehow that doesn't bother me. It's a historic accident that I was born in Long Beach, California. I loved to swim in the Pacific and to lie under the apricot tree reading fairy tales; all the same, I was just too hot too often growing up. Now I'm going to get to know the cold, as I've always dreamed of doing. I'm still thinking about Gerda's journey, still hearing the Danish in my mind. *Den vide verden.* The wide world.

I open the door of my cabin and a blast of winter snow rushes in. But, unlike Gerda, I'm dressed for my journey.

I have my shoes on. And two pairs of thick socks.

Revisiting Brideshead

Brideshead Revisited, by Evelyn Waugh

n the flyleaf of my copy of *Brideshead Revisited*— a blue Dell paperback, seventy-five cents—is written, in the flowery handwriting I thought elegant at age sixteen, "If I should die, think only this of me: / That there's some corner of a foreign field / That is for ever England." The same inscription appears in my *Penguin Book of English Verse*, in *The Mill on the Floss*, in the collected poems of Ernest Dowson and Keats and Wordsworth. Presumably I wrote it in my copy of *Pride and Prejudice*, too, and *The Once and Future King*, and the works of Tennyson, though I cannot check, since they all vanished long ago.

But *Brideshead Revisited*, to quote one of its most objectionable characters, *was* England to me—which is to say, nothing so mundane as a rainy island, the center of a vanishing empire, but a condition of heightened romance, the ultimate state of grace. In England, I was sure, people were not only wittier and more charming—that went without saying, any moviegoer knew as much—but gentler, finer, more honorable. They would never speak in loud, shrill voices or force themselves on anyone's attention or tell dirty jokes; their famous politeness was the expression of a genuine delicacy of feeling. They never bragged about their amazing heroism or their invincible decency during the Second World War. They believed in fair play rather than in competitiveness; they understood that principled failure was nobler than vulgar success.

I think I seriously believed that nobody in England ever lied or cheated (the characters in Dickens weren't real, anyway; they were just caricatures, like Popeye). Wickedness and cruelty did not exist among them; their very worst sin, like Mrs. Bennet's in *Pride and Prejudice*, was silliness (which gave rise to English wit). And their moral greatness was conflated, in my mind, with their superior refinement: in all of Berkshire, Hampshire, Gloucestershire, there were no cheerleaders with pom-poms, as there were in my suburban high school; no split-level houses with orange wall-to-wall carpet. Loveliness—it was such an English word, conjuring up sheep grazing peacefully on verdant hillsides, blue-and-white Wedgwood, ancient rose-covered cottages of honey-colored stone—was the order of the day.

At the time my fervor was reaching its peak—the mid-1960s—news of another, grittier England had long since arrived in America: the evils of the class system, that feudal leftover which kept a large segment of the population ruthlessly "in its place," had been exposed and attacked by some gentlemen known as the Angry Young Men. They in turn had been superseded, in the public eye, by the working-class Beatles, themselves at least moderately angry (well, John Lennon was) about their country's social hierarchies. London was in the midst of its swinging revolution; liberation was in the air. The rarefied England of my imagination was ceasing to exist even in English novels. It had become irrelevant, a matter for mockery, to the English themselves. Somehow, though, however much I read about the youthquake and the mods and the rockers, my private vision remained intact. After all, John Lennon wasn't only angry; he was witty, too, and charming: really quintessentially English in his way.

But *Brideshead Revisited* was on a higher plane altogether, the very highest of planes; it was the apotheosis of Englishness. Nothing could have been further from the crassness of suburban America than Waugh's elegiac tale of an aristocratic Catholic family possessed of such spiritual grace that their titles and estates seem like only the outward manifestations of their inner radiance.

It was impossible to imagine an American Sebastian Flyte—the youngest son of the family, the central presence (one cannot call him the hero exactly) of the first half of *Brideshead*, whose absence haunts the remainder of the book. Sebastian—Lord Sebastian—is blessed with an extraordinary romantic innocence; he is also "magically beautiful, with that epicene quality which in extreme youth sings aloud for love and withers at the first cold wind." At Oxford, he carries a teddy bear named Aloysius, whom he scolds and is scolded by in the most playful, charming, eccentric fashion. Sebastian is in flight (though it seems unlike Waugh to have made a deliberate pun) from, first, his family, and, second—the two are inextricably linked in his mind—his religion, whose mysteries are always overwhelmingly present, though he tries to turn his back on them by losing himself in worldly pleasures. One of his sisters believes that he has a religious vocation he is attempting to escape; certainly, despite his mischievous high spirits, the aura Waugh creates around him is that of a holy man.

As his pious mother increases her inexorable pressure on him—to take on adult responsibilities, to become an observant member of his faith—Sebastian retreats further and further into alcoholism. Finally, after many years of mournful exile abroad, he finds refuge as an underporter in a North African monastery, a gentle, melancholy figure with "little eccentricities of devotion, intense personal cults of his own."

The idea of someone too pure to live in the world, too ethereal and delicate to cope with harsh reality, seemed to me like the most exalted poetry. If you had asked me at the time whether the prince of Denmark or Sebastian Flyte was the more tragic figure, I would unhesitatingly have chosen Sebastian.

But there is another kind of romance, too, in *Brideshead*, almost though not quite as poignant. The narrator of the novel, Charles Ryder, whose intense but never explicitly sexual love for Sebastian at Oxford has provided all the major revelations of his youth—"to know and love one other human being is the root of all wisdom"—falls deeply in love, years later, with Sebastian's sister Julia. By this time, Charles, a painter of stately homes, is married to the obnoxious, worldly character who says that he *is* England to her; Julia, whose "Florentine Quattrocento" beauty is uncannily like Sebastian's, is also unhappily married, to a boorish former colonial. The lovers take up residence together at Brideshead, the Flytes' countryseat, which, like the family itself, is magically beautiful: "Here, as I passed through those arches and broken pediments to the pillared shade beyond and sat, hour by hour, before the fountain . . . I felt a whole new system of nerves alive within me, as though the water that spurted and bubbled among its stones was indeed a life-giving spring."

Ultimately, however, Charles is separated from Julia, as he was from Sebastian, by the mystery his "pagan" nature fails to comprehend: the pull of her religion, which years of willful apostasy cannot diminish. Her renunciation of mortal love for the love of God seemed to me the novel's crowning beauty; her impassioned monologue about the wrong she is doing by living with Charles without the Church's benediction was the rapturous high point of its eloquence:

> *Living in sin*, with sin, by sin, for sin, every hour, every day, year in, year out. . . . Mummy carrying my sin with her to church, bowed under it and the black lace veil, in the chapel; slipping out with it in London before the fires were lit; taking it with her through the empty streets. . . . Mummy dying with it, Christ dying with it, nailed hand and foot, hanging over the bed in the night-nursery . . . hanging year after year . . . hanging in the dark church where only the old charwoman raises the dust and one candle burns; hanging at noon, high among the crowds and the soldiers . . . hanging for ever; never the

cool sepulchre and the grave clothes spread on the stone slab,
never the oil and spices in the dark cave; always the midday
sun and the dice clicking for the seamless coat.

If *Brideshead* confirmed and heightened my reverence
for all things English, it also made Catholicism itself seem so
romantic that during the two years I was under its spell, I
constantly fantasized about converting, or even becoming a
nun. I did not, however, ask myself whether I believed in the
doctrines of the Church; that seemed irrelevant.

For years, the book glowed in my mind, but some instinct
warned me against trying to read it again; it was part of the
great romance of my youth. In my twenties, I lived in England for long stretches and discovered—partly through the
exasperated intercession of my English friends, who felt
hono(u)r-bound to point it out to me—that for all its glories,
it was as flawed as any other place. It seemed unnecessary to
forfeit any more illusions.

Then, in 1982, Granada produced its ten-hour version of
Brideshead, which was promptly transferred to American
television, and suddenly it became everybody's romance. It
was painful to see those characters translated into mere
flesh-and-blood people on the television screen. It was an
even worse affront that the actor playing Sebastian was ath-
letically stocky, with a pug nose, a blond thatch, and an imp-
ish grin. Didn't the people responsible for the production
understand *anything*? Didn't they know that Sebastian must
be ethereal and slender, with exquisitely fine features and
dark flowing hair?

More disturbing still, somehow, was the way the words that were about to be spoken kept flooding into my head. Most of the dialogue had been faithfully lifted from the book, and line after line came back to me a split second before it was uttered, a form of recovered memory I found so agitating I had to turn off the set. Perhaps it was because the words no longer had the same power over me. It was like meeting someone I'd been in love with years before and finding that all his little mannerisms, the traits that had once seemed so thrilling and precious, now left me unmoved.

Finally, more than a decade later—it had been thirty years since I first read the book—I was browsing through my bookshelves one evening, looking for something to take on an airplane the next day. I took down the little blue paperback and started reading.

Even the sternest critics of *Brideshead*, such as Edmund Wilson, have acknowledged that the first half, comic and elegiac by turns, is "quite brilliant." (The lament for lost innocence is one of the things the English have always done better than anyone else; from *Paradise Lost* to the "Immortality Ode" to *Peter Pan*, they have given voice to a great national yearning.) The portrait of Sebastian as a God-haunted dreamer is genuinely affecting; the humorous bits, like the war of wits between Charles and his sly, half-batty father, are some of the most brilliant things Waugh ever did, which, since he was a comic genius, is saying a lot. As I read on, I had a huge sense of relief. Though I could not, of course, feel the same intense rapture this time around (that was part of my youthful experience of novels; it would be ridiculous to expect it in my forties), at least I had not been mistaken. It was a wonderful book after all.

But when I arrived at the tale of Charles as an adult, things started to go badly wrong. There is, for example, the problem of the love between Charles and Julia, which is constantly described as perfect. They have never quarreled for a moment; there has never been "a day's coldness or distrust or disappointment." If that weren't enough to make one slightly skeptical, there is Waugh's unfortunate way of dealing with Charles's children, whom his discarded wife—annoyingly enough—feels he ought to see occasionally. Clearly, we are meant to regard this request as another example of the noxious world intruding on the lovers' idyll. Perhaps, too, Charles's fine disdain for his children's feelings is intended as a sign of his innately aristocratic nature, despite his middle-class origins. At times like this, Waugh seems to have a tin ear for ordinary human decency; he is so concerned with ecstatic modes of feeling and high religious obligations that he fails to realize it is in downright bad taste (vulgar in the ultimate sense of the word) to make Charles's indifference to his children a point of pride.

Then there is the increasingly purple prose—Julia's long soliloquy beside the fountain, which it is impossible to imagine any human being ever delivering, and the even longer soliloquy by her Byronic father, who has returned to England, after twenty years, to die in his ancestral home: "Those were our roots in the waste hollows of Castle Hill, in the brier and nettle; among the tombs in the old church and the chantrey where no clerk sings. . . . We were knights then, barons since

Agincourt, the larger honours came with the Georges. . . .
Julia's son will be called by the name his fathers bore before the
fat days; the days of wool shearing and wide corn lands," etc.,
etc. Waugh wrote the book in wartime, in 1944. The upper-
class England that, as a passionate middle-class snob, he had
revered and cherished was finished. *Brideshead* is his elegy
for a vanished world. But I don't think that entirely accounts
for the book's sheer unreality, its feverish melodrama.

Nor does it account for its failure as a serious portrayal of
religious experience, or—as Waugh himself called it—"an
attempt to trace the workings of the divine purpose in a pagan world." Waugh, who had converted to Catholicism fourteen years earlier, presents his religion as wholly a matter of
gorgeous rite and mystery. Nowhere is there any real suggestion that it has moral content, that it might have any relationship to human feeling or human conduct. Catholicism,
in this view, is simply the Higher Romance, complete with
solemn renunciations ("Here in the shadow, in the corner of
the stair—a minute to say good-bye") and dramatic deathbed
reconciliations with God.

There is something inherently adolescent—Wilson
called it "extravagantly absurd"—about the brood of roman
ticism found here. The worship of aristocratic glamour, the
inability to conceive of a love in which there is any disagree-
ment or strain, even the notion that Sebastian's incapacity to
deal with the world is a mark of his spiritual purity: all these
are adolescent constructs, which is perhaps why I loved the
book so much when I was sixteen. It was an adolescent's vision of love and innocence, even of suffering and redemp-

tion. It was uniformly beautiful without being in any sense true.

There is a great scene in *Brideshead*—perhaps the most successful in its second half—in which Anthony Blanche, a decadent aesthete whom Charles knew at Oxford but has not seen for many years, harangues him about his most recent exhibition. Charles has been to Central America to paint ruins in the jungle (it is on the return voyage that he meets Julia again and falls in love with her). Anthony has heard at a society luncheon that his old friend

> had broken away, my dear, gone to the tropics, become a Gauguin, a Rimbaud. You can imagine how my old heart leaped. . . . I wanted to dash out of the house and leap in a taxi and say, "Take me to Charles's unhealthy pictures" . . . and what did I find? I found, my dear, a very naughty and very successful practical joke. It reminded me of dear Sebastian when he liked so much to dress up in false whiskers. It was charm again, my dear, simple, creamy English charm, playing tigers. . . . Charm is the great English blight. It does not exist outside these damp islands. It spots and kills anything it touches. It kills love; it kills art; I very much fear, my dear Charles, it has killed *you.*

Whether or not that is true of England, I think it is true of *Brideshead*. If, on the one hand, Waugh has managed to make alcoholism and snobbery and adultery seem ever so charming, he has also made God seem charming, and love, and art. Though the whole book is a defense of a hierarchical society, he has somehow failed to create a hierarchy within it: all its elements are equally lovely, and therefore equally inconsequential.

Strangely, in his satirical masterpieces—*Decline and Fall*, *A Handful of Dust*—Waugh's moral vision is much sharper. In *Brideshead*, he seems to have fallen under the spell of his own shimmering, gorgeous creation in much the way I did when, at sixteen, I made the book my escape from distasteful reality. If, as I. A. Richards said, some people are "swoon readers," then perhaps some books are particularly swoon-worthy, and *Brideshead* is one of them. It's no wonder that one adolescent at least wanted to swoon right into it and never, ever wake up.

The Pursuit of Worldliness

The Charterhouse of Parma, by Stendhal

tendhal first came into my life through the impassioned offices of Dr. Floyd Zulli. Improbable as it may sound to a younger generation, this professor with dark-rimmed glasses, a crew cut, and a zeal for world literature had mesmerized our household and thousands like it into getting up at 6:30 a.m. and turning on the television set to catch his lectures on the novel in a program called *Sunrise Semester.* Many took the TV course for college credit, but my folks did it for old-fashioned enlightenment. When I think about my parents, lowly textile clerks with no more than high-school diplomas, setting the alarm early to hear a lecture and trying to keep up with the reading, I could weep.

In any case, Floyd Zulli (what a name! the name of a Hungarian charlatan) kicked off his course with an interesting choice, Stendhal's *The Red and the Black.* In our Brooklyn ghetto, this writer was not a given, like Dostoyevsky or Kafka. I was immediately drawn to the mystical sound of "Stendhal,"

an author with one name, like a magician (or a charlatan, likewise). Of course Zulli made it clear that his real moniker was Marie-Henri Beyle, but Beyle's invention of a new identity for himself appealed to me. I, slogging through the indignities of high school, had some self-invention in mind as well.

At college, though we read a few chapters of *Le rouge et le noir* in French, I decided to defer the pleasure of finishing it on my own. Also, by this time I had picked up a snobbish prejudice that the very popularity of *The Red and the Black* made it a little common, whereas *The Charterhouse of Parma* seemed to exude the aroma of a delicacy: literary caviar. So I began my education in Stendhal with his last great novel, *Charterhouse*. It was assigned for colloquium class, too, come to think of it; I had no choice in the matter.

Colloquium was a big deal at Columbia: you had to be interviewed to get in, and supposedly only the most brilliant students—highest grades, best academic minds—made the cut. In practice this meant I was thrown in with a bunch of dull premedical students seeking to become well-rounded and only a few humanities soul mates. To this disappointment was added my unspoken shame, because most of the other seniors were entering their second year in the seminar, whereas I had been rejected the year before for junior colloquium. It didn't help that in that first interview I'd dismissed Jean Giraudoux as a lightweight, only to discover while idly going through the Butler Library card catalog that one of my interviewers had done his doctoral dissertation on Giraudoux!

In those days I was forever provoking Columbia with my working-class defensiveness, sometimes intentionally, sometimes not. An intentional provocation, surely, occurred in the first semester of senior colloquium, when, instead of doing an analytical paper on *Rameau's Nephew*, I wrote a scampish Diderotian dialogue about the colloquium itself, sending up everyone in class, including the two professors, F. W. Dupee, a lion of the English department, and Richard Kuhns, a younger, tweedier man from Philosophy, who co-taught the class. They were not amused and demanded a substitute paper, which I never handed in. (Dupee forgave me, apparently. He was a dear man, a peach, sympathetic to rebellion, and a fine critic with a subtle prose style: how I could have twitted him so cruelly I'll never know.) My next paper would be on *The Charterhouse of Parma*, and this time I resolved to play by the rules.

The Charterhouse of Parma has been characterized by Richard Howard as "a miracle of gusto, brio, élan, verve, panache." I took to the book immediately and avidly, and it remains a rarefied pleasure. Why this rather recherché novel should have so delighted me at age twenty needs some background. I'd already been submitting the shape of my future sensibility to a gang of writers who specialized in analysis and paradox. I was powerfully drawn to Nietzsche (who loved Stendhal, saying: "The man was a human question-mark. . . . Objection, evasion, joyous distrust, and love of irony are signs of health"), Gide (who declared *The Charterhouse of Parma* his favorite French novel), and Dostoyevsky (my idol)—they had prepared me, with their psychological lineage. Also, I loved the comic novel: Fielding's cheeky addresses, Sterne's digressions, Diderot's sabotage of normal plot flow, Svevo's rationalizing narrator, Machado de Assis's sardonic, pithy style. What tickled me most, I think, was voice—the sound of outrageous candor cutting to the point, combined with a touch of irony insinuating that it could never be that simple.

In Stendhal, I found the exemplar of a spasmodic, abrupt voice whose very impatience signaled vitality. Where another writer might take paragraphs to prepare an insight, Stendhal would polish the business off with a terse epigram ("Courtiers, who have nothing to examine in their souls, notice everything"). His mind was so generously stocked that he could throw away ideas the way Bob Hope did one-liners. His paragraphs lacked topic sentences; or rather, they were all topic sentence, one atop the other. He dispensed with transitional sentences whenever it suited him and, by doing so, "predicted" in prose the Godardian jump cut I loved. "Let us skip ten years of progress and happiness" was his typically brazen shortcut. To leave out plodding intermediate steps, you need sophistication about the deep structure of narrative, supreme confidence in yourself, and an unimaginable faith in the audience's intelligence.

Stendhal wrote like a free man. Unconstrained by popular opinion, he wrote "to the happy few" (the oft-quoted final words of *Charterhouse*) and for an audience a hundred years hence who would appreciate him. I was that audience, I liked to think.

I was especially smitten with the early battle episodes, wherein Fabrizio, our Italian hero, voluntarily enlists in the French army. Barely seventeen years old, he runs away from home with a head full of romantic notions and an allegiance to his idol, Napoleon. As he scoots from one place to another, following dubious escorts, dodging bullets, having his horse stolen, trying to discover whether he has actually taken part in a battle, and encountering a pusillanimous army in full retreat (this is Waterloo, remember), Stendhal observes with comic regularity that Fabrizio does not understand in the least what is happening. Ah, to understand what is happening to you—the pattern underneath ephemeral events!

If I had to summarize in one word what I cherished about *The Charterhouse of Parma* and Stendhal, that word would be "worldliness." There was a mystique about worldliness that attracted me at twenty. Not for me the adolescent pulings of *The Catcher in the Rye*: if the price of entering adulthood was loss of innocence and the residues of childlike wonderment, I could not pay up quickly enough. Disenchantment was my goal. So when the worldly diplomat Count Mosca advises his adored Gina to marry an elderly man who can give her wealth in return for her title, we may be shocked at this nobleman pimping his beloved, but then we appreciate his grasp of circumstances. In the same practical manner, Mosca advises Fabrizio to enter the priesthood with an eye to making bishop: a strange choice for a libidinous young man, requiring years of patient execution, but one that makes sense in the *rouge et noir* context of nineteenth-century ambition. He also advises Fabrizio to take a mistress from a conservative family and to read in public only the stupidest right-wing newspapers. We are none of us romantic isolates; we are social animals, being watched by potential allies and enemies. Mosca is a realist: it does not bother him that he has been cuckolded by his wife, but it does bother him that she has embarrassed him by doing it with a political enemy.

To be worldly means to know that men and women are not angels, that they have vanities and vices that they seek to justify. Choderlos de Laclos, author of *Les liaisons dangereuses*, one of my favorite novels at the time (and still), certainly went further, depicting depravity as the common rule. The strategies that Valmont and Mme de Merteuil suggest for each other in *Les liaisons dangereuses* invoke sex as a game of chess to ward off boredom. Stendhal was more interested in demonstrating the realpolitik of court life; but in both cases it was reason, aligned with the recognition of appetite, that intrigued me. I found the same combination in the Marquis de Sade. Youth, being largely powerless, is often fascinated with evil forces. But the gothic never appealed to me, because, as much as wanting evidence of evil, I was listening for, craving, reasoned analysis—the sound of calm French logic—even when it took a hypertrophied form, as in Sade.

The Charterhouse of Parma and *Les liaisons dangereuses* swept through our family. They were read and discussed by me; my older brother, Lenny; and my sister Betty Ann, who was a year younger than I (our youngest sister, Joan, was still playing with dolls). Betty Ann in particular—dark, attractive, moody—was drawn to portraits of strong, independent-minded, active women: in adolescence, she modeled herself on the Duchess Sanseverina, Mme de Merteuil, and Billie Holiday. For Lenny and me, the duchess (Gina) was a fantasy ideal, an older woman of worldliness, beauty, and intelligence who we dreamed would take us under her wing. I found myself identifying (as did, I suspect, Stendhal) with Count Mosca, whose impressive overview of life cannot win him first place in the heart of his beloved Gina. She is much more taken with her nephew, that gilded youth, that heedless naïf, Fabrizio. Wherever he goes, women fall over themselves to please him. And even older men, like the bishop, are fond of him. Placing himself forever in danger, he is continually being rescued by the interventions of guardian angels, most notably his adoring aunt.

I did not begrudge Fabrizio his triumphs; but, though we were the same age, twenty, in no way did I identify with him. I was already seeing myself as the witty secondary, the one who would not get the girl, just as a few months later, when I read *Sentimental Education* for colloquium, I immediately identified not with the dreamy, aristocratic Frédéric but with his resentful, lower-middle-class pal, Deslauriers. (Possibly, I think, so did Flaubert. I wonder if this is a professional deformation: the writer, stuck at his desk, avenges himself on his dreamboat protagonist by condescending to or otherwise undercutting him.)

At Columbia, I had watched with fascination two of my classmates, Mitch and Jon, who seemed to me golden boys. I had befriended both. You might even say, in retrospect, that I'd had crushes on them, though I would have denied it. It seemed they were always plunging into complicated situations—being torn between several girls vying for their attention, between several spiritual or aesthetic paths—and then coming to me for advice. I simultaneously envied their success with women and felt superior, from my perch of ironic detachment. But why should I have been certain so early that I could not be a ladies' man? Cowardice, probably. I don't think being a ladies' man is ever a matter entirely of looks but, rather, of a certain receptivity to adventure and, with it, an incompleteness of self. A man with those qualities is often more enticing to women than a man who projects himself as a "finished portrait" (as I was already attempting to do). Gina cannot love Count Mosca with all her heart, because he is too cautious and aware of every consequence, while Fabrizio has the reckless, impetuous disregard of a sleepwalker, which she identifies with capacity for passion (rightly, it turns out, though his passion will be for Clélia, not for her).

I could never re-create my precise responses to Fabrizio or the novel after all these years were it not for the fact that I happened to keep my colloquium paper. Here it sits before me, typewritten on onionskin, with Professor Dupee's penciled comments—a shipwrecked sailor rescued from the ark of time. "Fabrizio, the Unconscious Hero." At the risk of being laughed at for exposing my undergraduate prose, I will quote:

> The unconscious hero was a favorite character of novelists in the eighteenth and nineteenth century. . . . The unconscious hero's ejection from the secure surroundings of his childhood into the larger world, his naïve attitudes confronted with obvious examples of evil, his near-passive participation in a string of marvelous incidents which thrust him into the path of danger and grotesque characters, and finally, his arrival at a stable position—was a formula employed in works as diverse as *Candide, Roderick Random, Tom Jones, Gulliver's Travels, Justine*, and *The Charterhouse of Parma*.
>
> The lack of great consciousness in a novel's protagonist seems to increase his susceptibility to coincidence. The rational, active, tragic hero in literature constructs his own destiny, and if he is defeated by fate the implication remains that he himself laid the groundwork for his failure. The unconscious hero, however, becomes much more controlled by the laws of chance.
>
> He is incredibly handsome, so much so that most people are immediately won over to him by his physical appearance; he is graceful, strong, courageous, and sufficiently proud of his honor to fight against personal attacks; he is naïve, gallant and susceptible to romantic notions; he is frequently passive. A character with these attributes is quite useful to the writer of an epic adventure novel, because the writer must be able to create a perpetual stream of incidents and plot twists. If the hero is handsome, then at any moment a woman may fall passionately in love with him, arouse her lover's jealousy and incite a duel.

In retrospect, it seems to me I was taking mocking revenge upon my popular, handsome friends. Though Mitch and Jon were both highly intelligent, my consolation was the prejudice that they were unconscious Fabrizios and I was the ever-alert Count Mosca. My dream was to become Stendhal, never his romantic hero.

The rest of the paper analyzed the many ways Stendhal explained Fabrizio's unconsciousness. For instance, the anti-clerical author blamed Catholicism, "the instruction given him by the Jesuits of Milan. That religion *deprives one of the courage to think of unfamiliar things*, and especially forbids *personal examination*, as the most enormous of sins; it is a step towards Protestantism." Or youth: "He was too young still; in his moments of leisure, his mind devoted itself with rapture to enjoying the sensations produced by the romantic circumstances with which his imagination was always ready to supply him. He was far from employing his time in study-ing with patience the actual details of things in order to dis-cover their causes."

I cited Fabrizio's unconscious cruelty toward his aunt, af-ter she has rescued him from prison, and went on to indict him: "His passion for Clélia ultimately leads to the death of his lover, their child, the Duchess and Fabrizio himself. Yet none of this tragedy would have occurred had Clélia and Fabrizio taken a rational course of action." (This is definitely a twenty-year-old talking!)

In the end, however, I gave Fabrizio his due by saying: "But if Fabrizio is led into situations of danger and eventual tragedy by his instincts, he is also elevated above the com-mon run of men. It is Fabrizio's reckless heroism which wins him the adoration of Gina; yet this heroism, as with every-

thing else about him, is of a peculiarly unconscious nature."
And to prove it, I ended by quoting Gina: "I love in him his
courage, so simple and so perfect that, one might say, he is
not aware of it himself."

In the next twenty years, I stockpiled Stendhal's books. Often,
going on vacation, when I wanted something I knew would
amuse me, I would pluck a title of his from the shelf. *The
Red and the Black* proved to be one of those special novels,
like *Vanity Fair*, whose vivacity and charm far exceed what
you might expect from a classic. I think it's Stendhal's best. I
read his lesser novels, such as the refined *Armance*, the slight
Lamiel, and the interminable *Lucien Leuwen*, which is interesting on every page but never comes to any point (it was left
unfinished, perhaps because Stendhal realized he was spin-
ning his wheels). I also read his Italian tales, such as "Vanina
Vanini," which have the economy of Kleist, if not the same
payoff. The tales did not stay with me; but the storyteller
remained good company throughout.

In the meantime, Bertolucci's *Before the Revolution* had
made a great stir: it was daring, youthful, formally inventive,
yet attached to the traditions of an older culture, including
Stendhal. The aura around *The Charterhouse of Parma* only
deepened with Bertolucci's film, which plays off that novel
in subtle ways, being set in Parma and featuring a beautiful
aunt who is romantically obsessed with her nephew.

Finally, I turned to Stendhal's "creative nonfiction" and
was enchanted again. *On Love*, his book-length meditation,

seemed an astonishing font of philosophy, reverie, and paradox: it made me want to write essays. For the moment, it ex-
cited me enough that I imitated the master with a chapter
called "Journal of Decrystallization" in my first novel, *Con-
fessions of Summer*. Later, when I had gravitated definitively
to the personal essay, I gobbled up his two autobiographical
texts, *The Life of Henry Brulard* and *Memoirs of an Egotist*.
The "I" in these books is one of his greatest characters: mischievous, Oedipal, pedantic, irascible, enthusiastic. I also
read his *Roman Journal*. By this time, Stendhal had become
for me one of those writers, like Montaigne or Borges, whose
sentences are incurably interesting, regardless of whether
the piece they are embedded in comes together.

Then I returned to where I started, and reread, several
weeks ago, *The Charterhouse of Parma*.

I am fifty-seven years old; in a few years I will be sixty! This
fact, which shakes me to the core, cannot help inspiring indifference in you, the reader. I completely understand your
refusal to be moved by my aging. I even applaud it. And in
part I feel it myself: Who cares? But I ask myself, What has
all this aging accomplished? It has lost me the ability to appreciate a literary masterpiece.

I can no longer read Kerouac for pleasure; Dostoyevsky
repels me. The Stendhal of the ruminations on love, travel,
and himself continues to act as a replenishment, but I find
Charterhouse tiresome. Not all of it, of course. I still love the
battle scenes, and the great interior monologues of Count

Mosca and Fabrizio in chapter 7, and Gina flinging herself into her nephew's arms. I still love much of the analytical psychology. But as a whole, it feels a little too willed, precious, artificial. That so much of the narrative exists in summary—which I once regarded as audacious—now seems vitiating. Stendhal dashed off *The Charterhouse of Parma* in fifty-two days, at the end of 1838, and the circumstances of its composition (or should I say performance?) show: in its penchant for summary, in its likeness to a single whoosh of sustained exhalation, in its tour-de-force bravura quality, but also in its repetitions and hasty summings-up.

Stendhal's recurrent potshots, such as using the warm-heartedness of his Italian characters to reproach French calculation, wear on my nerves. Count Mosca's long Machiavellian disquisitions on the inner workings of the court are no longer as fascinating this time around. It could be that worldliness itself, the initial attraction of *Charterhouse*, no longer possesses the same allure, the same meaning for me. I have it—or as much as I am going to have.

The book also feels like an uneasy commingling of two traditions: the French psychological novel and the Italian tale, with farcical elements of opera libretto and commedia dell'arte. In my youth I had accepted the mixture of genres as an enrichment; this time I balked, partly because I was less able or willing to submit to the story as a waking dream. Over the years I seem to have lost some of my youthful capacity to enter the mimetic/oneiric space of a novel; and this coincides with my becoming more drawn to essays, history, memoir. Call it mental hardening of the arteries.

I also now mistrust Stendhal's brief for romantic love. His skepticism is more credible to me than his romanticism. *The Charterhouse of Parma* plays as a conflict between reason and passion. Stendhal admired passion but, I think, didn't really believe in it. He needed it, though, to advance the plot, so that he wouldn't get bogged down again, as happened with *Lucien Leuwen*, in observation, without an engine (passion) to drive it. The same Stendhal who wrote the *Life of Rossini* turned to operatic passion as a convention. In *Charterhouse*, this inflatedly noble tale, he sought to reproach a commercial age. But he was on firmer ground with the scheming middle-class upstart Julien Sorel in *The Red and the Black* than with the aristocratic hunk Fabrizio.

The brio, the élan, the *sprezzatura* of *The Charterhouse of Parma* are an attempt to illustrate novelistically the charms of aristocracy. Now, Stendhal was not an aristocrat; though a man of the world, he had to be bluffing his posture here somewhat. I'm ashamed to say (it sounds so unworldly) that part of what put me off the novel this time was its class snobbery. We are told early on, doubtless with a trace of irony, that Fabrizio believes his high birth entitles him to a greater share of happiness than other men are entitled to. But Stendhal at times seems to swallow the notion of a highborn person's moral or aesthetic superiority. When Fabrizio kills a jealous actor, Giletti, who comes at him with a sword, all the enlightened characters treat this act as inconsequential, because the actor was riffraff. Stendhal's narrator himself says: "Actually the murder of Giletti was a trifle, and only political intrigue had managed to turn it into a matter of any importance." All right, so Stendhal was not a demo-crat, even if he was a liberal. But can he really have felt that murdering a human being meant nothing? Or was this his way of satirizing the solemnity of moralists? Either way, the absence of further clarification leaves me uncomfortable.

Later, when Fabrizio is being booked for this crime, we have the following exoneration by bloodlines: "During this brief exchange, Fabrizio stood patiently amid these police, showing the noblest expression [which] contrasted charm-ingly with the coarse appearance of the policemen around him." It would be one thing if Fabrizio were such a charm-ing character that the reader himself felt inclined to forgive him; but here we come to my central complaint. Fabrizio is a bore, a cipher, unfit to hold the focus of such a complex novel. His raptures by the lake, his mooning over Clélia in prison, all of these passages dragged for me.

How could I not have seen this when I was younger?

I went back and read my college paper. What impressed me was my earlier patience with Fabrizio. For all my underlying malice against this lucky pup, the younger me still accorded him the respect due a legitimate leading man. Rather than be-ing irritated, I was curious about why Stendhal should choose him as his narrative vessel, and I went to the trouble of de-veloping a literary thesis around it. What had happened to me over the years, that I'd gotten so much dumber? Was it that, with aging and balding, I no longer had even minimal patience for stories of privileged youths? Or had experience taught me that we were all golden boys and girls at moments; and thus the archetype had lost its morose fascination?

I was particularly taken with Fred Dupee's penciled comments on the first page: "Thorough and well reasoned essay—on a fruitful topic. I only think that you might distinguish more between F's 'unconsciousness' and the consequences of it for his temperament; his being able to 'live happily in the moment,' as Stendhal says. Isn't it this last that makes him great, rather than unconsciousness itself?" Living happily in the moment has proved not to be my forte. I think that even at twenty I suspected it would not be, and was already mounting defenses against the lack. Professor Dupee was pointing to this blind spot. Dupee himself was, I think it safe to say, bisexual in his longings, if not his practice. He had, in fact, a crush on my friend Jon, which the latter told me about. It may be that the homoerotically inclined retain more of a lifelong enchantment with the youthful Adonis figure, which would enable them to appreciate better the comedy of that superior older person, Gina, fainting in anguish at the indifference of Fabrizio. It may be that great artists, be they Mozart or Stendhal or Shakespeare, always possess something of the hermaphrodite in their character. I am just speculating here. In any case, Stendhal believed in Italy, *dolce far niente*, happiness, in a way I no longer could. To that extent, the novel had stopped working for me.

Nevertheless, because I knew I was wrong, I went back and read parts of it a third time. With pleasure. Taken a little at a time, like a poison or a homeopathic medicine, *The Charterhouse of Parma* remains delicious.

The Back of the Album

Sgt. Pepper's Lonely Hearts Club Band, by the Beatles

n June of 1967, when I was nine, my brother and I were farmed out to summer camp in Vermont. In those days you went off with a fully packed trunk and spent more or less the whole summer far from home. You were not allowed to bring anything that connected you with civilization, not even a transistor radio to follow the baseball season. But late one morning in July, I heard by chance the opening bars of a record that had somehow arrived in camp from civilization's very epicenter. I had been on my contented way from archery, in the upper field, to woodworking, in the barn—a day that could just as easily have been taking place in 1947, because none of the traditional forms of a boy's camp life had yet changed, as everything about the way we thought and dressed and did things was to change after 1967—when from the barn's shuttered hayloft the electric sound of *Sgt. Pepper's Lonely Hearts Club Band* bolted through the clean, sunny air.

The counselors' lounge was seedy and inaccessible, an outpost of adult mysteries. The physical presence of the new Beatles album up there behind closed doors created a charged atmosphere I will never forget. I was almost sick with the sheer nerve of it. I remember feeling pierced by the words—*It was twenty years ago today*—and in that first instant of listening in, the shock of the new Beatles record combined with the prestige of the counselors' lounge to produce an alternate reality.

Archery? Woodworking? I couldn't have cared less. Of course I couldn't give them up, either. I loved archery, I wanted to impress my parents with a Bowman's Medal, and as that summer went on—the Summer of Love, it turned out—I felt the clear, straight lines of my boyhood becoming blurred in a way I did not fully understand.

I knew a little about the Beatles already. I owned two Beatles records (*A Hard Day's Night* and *Beatles '65*), and when I was six and my brother seven, we had owned Beatles wigs. They were oddly shaped, scruffy thatches of synthetic black hair that fit over our heads like ladies' bathing caps and didn't look anything like the real thing. We didn't mind— these were *Beatles* wigs, and there was something deliciously insubordinate about wearing them. Years later, when I studied a passage of Milton that described Adam and Eve's childlike rebellion in Eden, I had a pang of giddy joy that reminded me of the liberation I had felt each time I pushed my scalp through the wig's hairy opening.

This new album was different, more complicated. It was no longer just a release of youthful energy; there was an elegiac tone in both the words and the music, and that was what made me feel I was entitled to their hidden truths. The previous summer my parents had sat my brother and me down for an important talk. I knew before the word "separation" knifed into our living room that it really meant divorce. "Nothing will change," they said. "We both love you very much." It was my mother who for years afterward would say, "We're still a family."

The message of *Sgt. Pepper* was that things were not as they appeared, which made me, I felt intuitively, the perfect student of its puzzles. Every day, it seemed, additional information about *Sgt. Pepper* came into circulation: a 20,000 Hz tone, audible only to dogs, had been recorded backward into the inner groove at the end of the album's British version. It was said that dogs all over England were going bananas when tonearms on hi-fi sets failed to pick up automatically and instead drifted into the subversive inner groove of *Sgt. Pepper*. Every night, it seemed, the two counselors in my cabin discussed the album, quietly debating shades of meaning we didn't understand; I recall one of them telling the other that the reverberating piano chord at the end of the record (E major, held for forty-two seconds) gave him cold chills because it was *supposed* to make you think of a nuclear explosion.

It almost didn't matter that we weren't allowed to listen to the album, let alone hear the chiller chord that ended "A Day in the Life" or the 20,000 Hz dog alarm. The mystification that surrounded the album had as much to do with the art on the cover as it did with the record itself. Marijuana plants, for example, could be clearly seen in the photographic tableau on the *Sgt. Pepper* cover—*real pot plants*, daringly placed in plain sight at the Beatles' feet, or so the counselors said.

One night they brought the album around for inspection. We each had a turn with it. The infamous tableau was as densely woven as a tapestry; it was hard to know where to look. Under the big blue Northern England sky, tiers of cutout faces, cloth figures, waxworks, ferns, potted palms, garden ornaments, and sculptural busts were arrayed around the flesh-and-blood Beatles, who, tiger-bright in military-band regalia and holding brass and wind instruments instead of electric guitars, stood poker-faced behind a circusy Lonely Hearts Club Band drum skin. We tried to name faces in the crowd behind the band. Somebody pointed out Sonny Liston. There, too, was Marlon Brando from *The Wild One*, a popular poster image on the bedroom walls of older brothers in my neighborhood. I recognized the early Beatles as Madame Tussaud's wax figures, and I knew Bob Dylan—he was a folk singer. All else was unknown to me. I recall turning over the album. There, vibrating in black print on a Chinese-red background, were the words.

It's hard to remember now what this meant then. To paraphrase Kenneth Tynan's remark about how *Citizen Kane* changed filmmaking: *Sgt. Pepper's Lonely Hearts Club Band* revolutionized pop music as the airplane revolutionized warfare. Until *Sgt. Pepper*, the pop single had dominated the recording industry, each 45 rpm record comprising two songs, the hit tune on side A, a lesser song on side B. Pop singles were marketed in a plain sleeve with no sign that the lyrics were to be treated as anything more than bubble gum, chewed once and tossed away.

From *Introducing the Beatles* in 1963 to *Revolver* in 1966, the Beatles had supplemented the traditional release of new hit singles with annual appearances of two-sided LPs, the covers of which, though increasingly brash and inventive, gave no warning of what *Sgt. Pepper* would unleash. Inside and out, everything about the new record was narrative. It was bursting to tell a story. The Beatles made their regular instruments, from bass guitar to drums, sound like voices that had something fresh to say while making the harpsichord and the fiddle, as well as classical instruments from India, seem integral to the most far-out aspirations of rock 'n' roll. It was the first rock album to insert orchestral scoring for narrative effects—one of many ways in which *Sgt. Pepper* was created more in the manner of filmmaking than by the conventions of the music industry. And if the recording processes devised in the Abbey Road studios gave *Sgt. Pepper* the aura of a mod film, the sumptuous packaging that the Beatles insisted upon clothed the record in its most characteristic quality: readability. Here was the first album ever to publish its lyrics on the back. The songs told a story that was connected by a theme and that could be read cover to cover.

After that first eager glimpse in camp, I bought the record, with my mother, at Sam Goody's, on a visit to Manhattan.

Back in our living room, at the exact middle of the sofa, where my mother's gay designer friend sat each of us in turn to demonstrate the brand-new effects of stereo (a scientific moment that my father would previously have husbanded us through), I settled into a habit of sitting cross-legged and alone, ostentatiously studying *Sgt. Pepper*'s words without playing the stereo at all. It was a deliberate act to *read* the Beatles without the music. Using eye instead of ear to ransack the lyrics for their hidden adult meanings turned even a ten-year-old into a seeker of ambiguity, an investigator of the imagination, a devotee of poetry. I had no musical ability then or now, and being given the words on a Chinese-red platter was like being rewarded in school with a period of free play. The literariness of Lennon and McCartney was just my speed. Looking-glass ties? Cellophane flowers that tower over your head? A hole that needs fixing? Where had I heard this before? Of course: Alice on the riverbank, Alice down the Rabbit-Hole, Alice in the Garden of Live Flowers.

Sgt. Pepper seemed nothing less than an *Alice in Wonderland* for the brave new psychedelic world. Everything in Pepperland was reversed, just as in Lewis Carroll's mirror-crazy Wonderland. The Lonely Hearts Club Band was "in style" one moment, "out of style" the next. In "Getting Better," things got better because they could get no worse. In "Fixing a Hole," it really didn't matter "if I'm wrong / I'm right." Life in Pepperland flowed two ways at once: "within you and without you."

Curiouser and curiouser! The most forward-looking recording in the history of rock music began by looking back to a day twenty years in the past. Recorded tracks, when reversed and played back, had new and sometimes sexual meanings. The cover image was full of reversals: old heroes were young again; celebrities were "lonely hearts"; the most popular rock group in the world had become a small-time brass band. Look in the tableau's foreground, where the hottest name in 1960s show business—BEATLES—was spelled out in a deliberately parochial form of display: municipal flower-bed lettering.

My true experience of *Sgt. Pepper* was as a reader. The wordplay was no more complicated than that which I had adored in Edward Lear's nonsense verse or in O. Henry's grifter stories, which I was reading in sixth-grade English. M. C. Escher, whose magic realism I encountered in math class, thanks to a brilliant and iconoclastic teacher, also showed that things were not as they seemed. The Beatles were asking the same question: What's wrong with this picture? Over and over, I read the album, trying to decode the tapestry on the front and the strange, spangled words on the back.

The Beatles had written songs that set out to be *not* understandable. *Sgt. Pepper* was a world in which, instead of receiving clear-cut statements, you projected your own dream onto a cloud. It was like Zen: the song *was* the question. You had to go through a process of self-emptying before you could absorb the answer. But the album's organizing principle, its thought-out-edness, took you . . . where? Back to itself. The Beatles coded their imagery, as all Romantic poets had, so that the younger generation, once it thought it had answered the riddle, could feel safe in its knowingness.

Sgt. Pepper belonged to a genre evergreen to adolescents: If you get it right, you will understand it, but the deeper truth is always one more magnification beyond where your non-dreaming mind can see.

As a boy, I thought the Beatles were the suave, avant-garde leaders of the culture. Whatever they wore in the early 1960s—Chelsea boots, mop haircuts, collarless jackets— everyone wore. By 1967, trapped by worldwide fame, they weren't so much leaders of the culture as hostages to its hot center. *Sgt. Pepper* shows them to be the spokesmen for an age that now seems nearly as quaint and faraway as Dickens's London. The Beatles didn't invent the New, as I thought; they invented an attitude through which to picture the New and the Old simultaneously. The costumes they chose for their *Sgt. Pepper* alter egos were takeoffs not just on the British imperial past but on the swinging London of 1967, when kids flocked to Carnaby Street and the King's Road to buy recycled police capes and brass-buttoned military coats at boutiques with names like I Was Lord Kitchener's Valet, which was also the title of a pop song by the New Vaudeville Band ("Winchester Cathedral" was their big single). Its chorus went:

> *Oh Lord Kitchener, what a to-do,*
> *Everyone is wearing clothes that once belonged to you.*
> *If you were alive today I'm sure you would explode,*
> *If you took a stroll down the Portobello Road.*

Rereading *Sgt. Pepper* thirty-five years later, I sat down in my office in Washington, D.C., with the scuffed album from Sam Goody's—it's been marooned for years with the rest of my records in a summer house that still has a record player. In my office, the only way to listen to music is on a compact disc inserted into the Microsoft Windows Media Player. Although I've updated most of the music of my youth with CDs, *Sgt. Pepper* is one of the albums that look so ridiculous in the miniature form (*Woodstock* is another: more than 6 square feet of visual material shrunk to 4¾ by 5½ inches of plastic casing sealed by the most infuriating packaging ever invented) that I haven't had the stomach to replace the original.

I scanned the back of the record cover, where five newspaper-column-size lines of black type still pulled me right in with the opener: "It was twenty years ago today, / Sgt. Pepper taught the band to play." I wanted to fall right back into the audience—to "sit back and let the evening go." But the lines were hard to read, and not just because the record inside the cover had rubbed a white circle onto the printed surface, erasing entire words. The lyrics are in my memory anyway. I didn't need to see them in print, because they alighted automatically, almost too quickly, on my inner ear. It was as if I had written them myself, and therefore could no longer lay claim to what happens only once during the initial excitement of creation: an awakening to life itself. Coming from within, predigested and reconstituted, instead of fresh and new from without, the words had calcified.

What rereading without music did allow me to see, however, was how concrete a place Pepperland actually is, and how much the Beatles' cloudlandish, countercultural effects needed the solid institutions, traditions, and even architecture of the receding Empire—"all that Trafalgar Square stuff," as John Osborne, England's brash young playwright of the 1950s, referred to the country's crippling nostalgia. Hallowed British scenes and settings in "Lucy in the Sky with Diamonds"—"a boat on a river," "a bridge by a fountain," "a train in a station"—are blown apart and repatterned by "tangerine trees," "rocking horse people," "plasticine porters," a "girl with kaleidoscope eyes." Every bit of color-saturated 1967 psychedelia comes alive because of the contrast with images of drab, gray postwar England.

At John Lennon's direction, the record's brilliant producer, George Martin, created the swirly, Victorian, and very English effects in the sawdust circus world of "Being for the Benefit of Mr. Kite!" Martin found recordings of old-fashioned steam organs, then scissored the tape into fifteen-inch segments, instructing Geoff Emerick, the recording engineer, to toss the lengths of tape into the air, pick them up, and resplice the bits into a new whole. That kind of Dadaist approach, while emblematic of the experiments that made *Sgt. Pepper* a mirror image of its time, could work musically only within the formal structure that Lennon and McCartney and Martin actually felt most comfortable inside. The lyrics of "Mr. Kite" may have sounded far-out to the ear in 1967, but "a splendid time is guaranteed for all" and the rest were sentences transposed verbatim from an 1843 circus poster that John Lennon had bought in an antiques shop in Sevenoaks, Kent.

Throughout *Sgt. Pepper*, English place-names (Bishops-gate; the Isle of Wight; Blackburn, Lancashire), British institutions (the old school; teatime; the House of Lords; the English army; the Royal Albert Hall), and English types (the grandchildren, Vera, Chuck, and Dave; Mr. Kite; the Hendersons; the man from the motor trade; Rita, the meter maid) are presented alternately as extensions of British greatness or as fading rays in the imperial sunset. The album's themes are anchored, more than I realized, in a period when England was looking back—part wistfully, part skeptically—to a world in which, more often than not, the "English Army had just won the war," although the 1967 narrator of "A Day in the Life" can remember the Empire's glory only from seeing it in a movie. The "twenty years ago today" that seems to invite the audience of a brass-band concert to recall an earlier, better time is actually pinpointing 1947 as the date from which the rest of the "show" follows—a year when Great Britain, lately in command of one-quarter of the world's landmass, was coming to terms with its decline. Awash in historical nostalgia for what had been, the English could easily recognize the symbols in John Osborne's bitter play *The Entertainer*, in which a collapsed music-hall player says, "Don't clap too loud, it's a very old building," a reference less to anything architectural than to the weakening of England itself.

The Beatles, grandchildren of Victorians, understood in

their twenties that they were witnessing the end not just of English folk arts—such as the music-hall variety show and the brass bands that had played green parks in every stronghold of the Empire—but of something significant about the English character. Their lives had begun during the last crucial test of the British people. The births of Richard Starkey in July of 1940 and John Lennon in October of 1940 and Paul McCartney in June of 1942 and George Harrison in February of 1943 coincided with England's darkest but finest hours. Hitler's blitzkrieg, the Nazi seizure of Paris, the fall of France, the collapse of the Chamberlain government, the rise of Churchill, the bombing of England, and the Battle of Britain all took place in the five months before John Winston Lennon's mother and aunt gave him a middle name inspired by Churchillian greatness. Twenty-five years later, in January 1965, Sir Winston's death and state funeral marked the final organizing moment of Britain's decline and the full flowering of Victorian nostalgia.

By 1967, the Beatles, driving force of the New and the Now, stood on the infamous cover of *Sgt. Pepper* like the gatekeepers of history. They had learned from their brief lives as world-renowned celebrities that things were not always as they appeared to be. In *The Beatles Anthology*, the millennial recounting of Beatles history by the Beatles themselves, Paul McCartney notes that "what we were saying about history [was that] all history is a lie, because every fact that gets reported gets distorted." Every kind of falsehood and misinterpretation had by then been reported about the Beatles and their music; untruth had freed them to create their own narrative, choose their own heroes, reinvent history.

Behind them, in a collage meant to illustrate their sense of the precise present moment of 1967, stood their hand-picked representatives of the collective cultural past. Into this pantheon the Beatles elevated a host of American movie stars and comedians, along with gurus and yogis, writers and painters (though not many musicians), Liverpool soccer heroes, and some seemingly conventional British figures whose lives contained surprise twists, such as the writer Aldous Huxley, who had experimented with mescaline and LSD in the early 1950s. Although the fictitious military bandleader Sergeant Pepper appeared only as a handout that came with the album—on a square of cardboard that also included bonus mustaches, badges, sergeant stripes, and other paraphernalia—I was interested to learn that there had been a real-life figure named Pepper: one of the many retired army officers of the British Raj in India who used their military ranks when playing for the local cricket team. Sergeant Pepper played for Uttar Pradesh.

Peering into the cover tableau now, I notice that the famous marijuana plants were, of course, nothing but greenery—a spiky houseplant whose Latin name, *Peperomia*, was another inside joke. I look at John, Ringo, Paul, and George, and see them consciously distancing themselves from the viewer. The band is photographed through a filter, with a deep-focus lens, and there's an extreme, almost death-like stillness on every surface. After the fantastic energy of their first five years, the Beatles are stepping back into the depths of time.

The atmosphere of mourning that fanatical fans inferred from the *Sgt. Pepper* tableau, which they believed contained a set of clues to the unannounced death of Paul McCartney, is, in a more real sense, a eulogy to lost childhood. The four young men on that record have no idea how, or even if, they are going to grow up, and if they do, how they will ever stay together as a band. Standing among the totems of their Liverpudlian Eden, pantomiming the gestures of a dying Empire, the Beatles were taking a first step out of their dizzyingly successful unadult lives and looking back to the solid England of Lennon's and McCartney's boyhood dreaming.

I had a similar feeling of deliberate distance in a bookstore the other day, when I noticed that Paul McCartney had printed some of the *Sgt. Pepper* lyrics (among others from the Beatles songbook) in a spotlessly dust-jacketed volume of poetry—as if, in other words, they weren't songs and really *had* been poetry all along. I picked up the tidy white book and tried to read the familiar words in the state of aural blankness it demanded. But some right-brain part of me kept letting in the music. Great big gusts of studio instrumentation blew into Sir Paul's spotless white Parnassian tent, ruining his sherry party. It was an odd reaction: when I was a boy, I read these lyrics on the back of the album as poetry, whereas now, dressed up in white tie and tails, they seemed to have *lost* their poetry. Published formally, *Sgt. Pepper*'s words no longer looked excitingly Now; they looked very Then.

During my preteen and teen years, most records entered my system for a while; I had favorite songs for various moods—an up song, a down song, a daydreaming song, a rebel song—and I memorized them all. After a season or two, those songs would pass out of me, and the record itself would remain a fixed piece of a fixed time in the past, part of my increasingly obsolete vinyl collection, an artifact of a lost age. *Sgt. Pepper*—the name as an abstraction; the image I carry in memory of its cover; even the original object itself, with the outline of the record within visible as a rubbed white circle on the cardboard without—remains in and with me, like a surgical plate connecting halves of a broken bone. *Sgt. Pepper's Lonely Hearts Club Band* had healing power, and in the summer of 1967 I needed something I couldn't have found in the tourniquet instructions in the *Boy Scout Handbook*. The Bowman's Medal I brought home from camp, which I thought would somehow change everything, seemed as theatrical and obsolete as the medals on the Beatles' military tunics.

After my father left my mother, she always awoke at five in the morning and lay in bed, thinking that he would come to his senses, walk out on the woman for whom he had walked out on her, and return home, to his side of the bed, where he belonged. So far as I know, my father had no intention of ditching my stepmother or her children, with whom he had formed a second family; and when it turned out that my mother wasn't going to choose a permanent replacement for Dad's side of the bed, I began to spend as much time as I could away from my own bed, too. I used to daydream myself into other families, and some of them actually took me in and let me live, without pauses, in the kind of extended living and eating plan that the early 1970s seemed to specialize in.

If the melody of "She's Leaving Home" now sounds melodramatic almost to the point of parody, I can still read in the words the strangely disembodied feeling my nine-year-old self tried on when I first encountered the song: Was this how it felt to have no home? To abandon and be abandoned? The story of my house and the household in the song did not match, but since my mother's day always began at five o'clock, the hour of the day's start in the song, and the hour before which I took some of my own exits from Eden, the lament of the refrained farewell—*bye bye*—still squeezes my heart.

ABOUT THE CONTRIBUTORS

KATHERINE ASHENBURG has been a producer at the Canadian Broadcasting Corporation and the arts and books editor of the Toronto *Globe and Mail*. She frequently writes about travel for *The New York Times*. Her most recent book is *The Mourner's Dance: What We Do When People Die*; her next one is *Clean*, a social history of bathing. Ashenburg lives in Toronto.

SVEN BIRKERTS is the author of five books of essays and a memoir, *My Sky Blue Trades: Growing Up Counter in a Contrary Time*. A member of the core faculty of the Bennington Writing Seminars, he also edits the journal *Agni*, based at Boston University. He has recently completed a book of essays on rereading the formative novels of his life, as well as a short book on the craft of memoir. Birkerts lives with his wife, Lynn, and their two children, Mara and Liam, in Arlington, Massachusetts.

ALLEGRA GOODMAN, a former member of *The American Scholar*'s editorial board, is the author of two collections of short fiction, *The Family Markowitz* and *Total Immersion*, and two novels, *Kaaterskill Falls* (a finalist for the National Book Award) and *Paradise Park*. A recipient of a Whiting Award and a Salon Magazine Award for fiction, Goodman has been named one of America's best writers under forty by *The New Yorker*. Her new novel, *Intuition*, will be published in 2006. She lives in Cambridge, Massachusetts.

VIVIAN GORNICK is the author of a memoir, *Fierce Attachments*; two essay collections, *Approaching Eye Level* and *The End of the Novel of Love* (a National Book Critics Circle Award finalist); and a guide to literary nonfiction, *The Situation and the Story: The Art of Personal Narrative*. She lives in New York City.

PATRICIA HAMPL is a Regents Professor at the University of Minnesota, a member of the permanent faculty of the Prague Summer Program, and a MacArthur Fellow. Her most recent book, *I Could Tell You Stories*, was a National Book Critics Circle Award finalist. Her prose works include the memoirs *A Romantic Education* and *Virgin Time* as well as *Spillville*, a meditation on Antonín Dvořák's 1893 visit to Iowa. Hampl's next book is *The Silken Chamber*, a study of the odalisque in Western art; her essay on rereading Katherine Mansfield will appear in it as one of several portraits of writers and artists in the South of France when Matisse was painting his Orientalist figures there. She lives in St. Paul.

PICO IYER is the author of several books about the romance between cultures, including *Video Night in Kathmandu*, *The Lady and the Monk*, *The Global Soul*, and *Abandon*. Born in Oxford to Indian parents, he was raised in England and California and now lives in Japan. His most recent book is *Sun After Dark*.

JAMIE JAMES is a native of Texas who has lived in Indonesia since 1999. He is the author of two novels, *Andrew and Joey: A Tale of Bali* and *The Java Man*. He has also published several nonfiction books, including *The Music of the Spheres*. A travel writer and critic, James has been the American arts correspondent for *The Times* of London and an art critic for *The New Yorker*. He and his partner recently moved from Jakarta to Bali to open a restaurant in the coastal village of Seminyak.

DIANA KAPPEL SMITH has been a writer, a botanist, a farmer, a painter, an illustrator, and a landscape designer. She is the author of three books of essays: *Wintering*, *Night Life: Nature from Dusk to Dawn*, and *Desert Time: A Journey Through the American Southwest*. Born in Connecticut, she now lives in Arizona.

ARTHUR KRYSTAL is an essayist and screenwriter. He is the editor of *A Company of Readers: Uncollected Writings of W. H. Auden, Jacques Barzun, and Lionel Trilling* and the author of *Agitations: Essays on Life and Literature*, a finalist for the 2003 PEN/Spielvogel-Diamonstein Award for the Art of the

Essay. Although his next book is titled *Who Speaks for the Lazy?—and Other Essays*, Krystal somehow managed to co-write the film *Thick as Thieves*, starring Alec Baldwin and Rebecca De Mornay, and is currently developing a film project on the early-nineteenth-century boxer Tom Molineaux. He lives in New York City.

PHILLIP LOPATE has championed the personal essay as the editor of *The Art of the Personal Essay* and the author of four collections: *Bachelorhood, Against Joie de Vivre, Portrait of My Body*, and *Getting Personal: Selected Writings*. His other books include *Waterfront: A Journey Around Manhattan*; *Totally Tenderly Tragically*, a collection of film criticism; and *Being with Children*, an account of his experiences as a writer-in-the-schools. Lopate is the John Cranford Adams Professor at Hofstra University and a member of the graduate faculty of M.F.A. programs at Columbia, the New School, and Bennington. His awards include fellowships from the Guggenheim Foundation, the National Endowment for the Arts, and the New York Public Library's Center for Scholars and Writers. He lives in Brooklyn with his wife, Cheryl, and their daughter, Lily.

DAVID MICHAELIS is the author of *N. C. Wyeth: A Biography*, winner of the 1999 Ambassador Book Award for Biography, given by the English-Speaking Union of the United States. His previous books include a collection of biographical sketches, *The Best of Friends*. Michaelis's work has appeared in *Vanity Fair, Condé Nast Traveler, American*

Heritage, and *The New York Observer*, for which he regularly reviews books; he is currently working on a biography of Charles M. Schulz. He lives in New York City.

DAVID SAMUELS has written about atom bombs, dog tracks, anarchists, rappers, forgers, demolition men, and religious visionaries for *Harper's Magazine* (of which he is a contributing editor), *The New Yorker*, and other publications. He and his wife live in Brooklyn, next to a mosque.

LUC SANTE is the general editor of the Library of Larceny and the author of *Low Life: Lures and Snares of Old New York*, *Evidence*, and *The Factory of Facts*. He has been the recipient of a Whiting Award, a Guggenheim Fellowship, an Award in Literature from the American Academy of Arts and Letters, and a Grammy (for album notes). Sante teaches writing and the history of photography at Bard College, and lives in Ulster County, New York.

VIJAY SESHADRI was born in India and grew up in the Midwest. He is the author of two collections of poetry, *The Long Meadow* (winner of the James Laughlin Award) and *Wild Kingdom*. His poems, essays, and reviews have appeared in *The New Yorker*, *The Threepenny Review*, *The Paris Review*, and other publications. Seshadri teaches at Sarah Lawrence College and lives in Brooklyn with his wife and son.

BARBARA SJOHOLM is the author of *The Pirate Queen: In Search of Grace O'Malley and Other Legendary Women of the Sea.* Her work has appeared in *The New York Times*, *Smithsonian*, and *Slate*, among other publications. Under the name Barbara Wilson, she is the author of *Blue Windows: A Christian Science Childhood* as well as a detective series about a translator-sleuth named Cassandra Reilly. One of the Reilly mysteries, *Gaudí Afternoon*, won a British Crime Writers' Association Award and became a film, shot in Barcelona, that starred Judy Davis and Marcia Gay Harden. Sjoholm has translated several books from Norwegian, including the stories of Cora Sandel, for which she won a Columbia Translation Center Award. Sjoholm is currently at work on a travel narrative about northern Scandinavia in winter. She lives in Seattle.

EVELYN TOYNTON is the author of the novel *Modern Art*. Her articles, essays, and reviews have appeared in *The Atlantic Monthly*, *The Threepenny Review*, *The New York Times Book Review*, *The Times Literary Supplement*, and other publications. Not long after completing the essay in this volume, she moved to Norfolk, England. She is at work on a second novel.

MICHAEL UPCHURCH is the author of the novels *Air*, *The Flame Forest*, and *Passive Intruder*. His reviews have appeared in *The New York Times Book Review*, *The Washington Post*, the *Chicago Tribune*, and the *San Francisco Chronicle*. His short fiction has appeared in *Christopher Street*, *Glimmer Train*, and the *Carolina Quarterly*. Since 1998 he has been the book critic for *The Seattle Times*. He lives with his partner, the film critic John Hartl, in Seattle.

ACKNOWLEDGMENTS

I would like to thank Jean Stipicevic and Sandra Costich, of *The American Scholar*, for shepherding these essays through their original publication, and me through an editorship that would have faltered without their kindness; Bill Whitworth for giving good advice; Robert Lescher for being the perfect literary—and I mean *literary*—agent; Jonathan Galassi and Annie Wedekind for offering this book sanctuary and guidance; Jonathan Lippincott for making it beautiful; George Colt for editing, reading, criticizing, appreciating, and galvanizing; and John Bethell for showing me, over the last thirty-five years, that whether one is distinguishing between "which" and "that," between a so-so typeface and an exquisite one, or between an uneven draft and a polished piece, editing matters.

A.F.